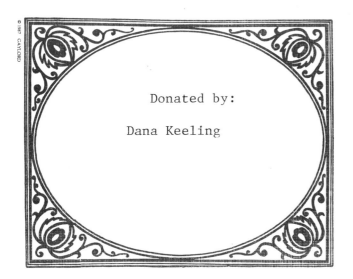

D0857360

DESIGNER'S ▮ GUIDE TO

color

2

Introductory Essay by James Stockton

Chronicle Books   San Francisco

First published in the United States 1984 by
Chronicle Books
275 Fifth Street
San Francisco, CA 94103

Printed in Japan.

Haishoku Jiten by Ikuyoshi Shibukawa
and Yumi Takahashi
Copyright © 1984 by Kawade Shobo
Shinsha Publishers

Library of Congress
Cataloging in Publication Data
Main entry under title:

Designer's guide to color. II.

Based on: Haishoku jiten by Ikuyoshi
Shibukawa and Yumi Takahashi, 1984.
1. Color in art.   2. Color.   3. Color—
Psychological aspects.   I. Stockton, James.
II. Shibukawa, Ikuyoshi. Haishoku jiten.
ND1488.D475 1984   701'.8   84-21482
ISBN 0-87701-340-3

10   9   8

Introduction

This second volume of *Designer's Guide to Color* is an extension of the first book, a careful, thorough look at more complicated color examples than were treated before. While the first book was basic and clinical, this one deals with the more personal, emotional aspects of color.

In this book, colors have been grouped together—pastels through deep tones as the pages progress. At the bottom of each page are two color squares with polka dots. These demonstrate how shape and size relationships affect color. And from page 78 to the end of this book, the possible combinations of color become interestingly complex by being presented in groups of three.

The adjectives used in the table of contents are for the reader's convenience and are an attempt to qualify the colors presented. Most of the terms are standard enough to be self-explanatory; however, the following terms are used in these specific ways: *Bright*—intense, light valued, transparent; receiving their brightness from the clean whiteness of the paper (much as a watercolor might). See pages 28 through 31. *Brilliant*—intense, strong pigment; a reflected color (more like an oil painting). See pages 36 and 37. *Medium*—soothing and subtle. See pages 76 and 77. Deep—rich and elegant. See pages 52 through 55. *Dark*—similar to deep but with much more black added to the colors. See pages 70 and 71. *Subdued*—grayed through either the addition of black, white, or a neutralizing complementary color. See pages 66 through 69. *Concentrated*—intense with strong hue, value, and intensity all combined. See pages 56 through 59. *Clear*—free of graying qualities; can probably be found on the basic color wheel. See volume one.

Short anecdotes accompany the color combinations. They are sometimes instructional, sometimes an attempt to articulate the motives for combining the colors. They may stimulate ideas and suggest extended uses of original combinations.

As in volume one, the colors in this book are produced by combining tint values—that is, screen values—of the four basic printing process colors. Each color is accompanied by the numbers designating those values, and abbreviated designations for the four colors are given with the percentages: Y stands for yellow, M for magenta, C for cyan, and BL or K for black.

To achieve strong areas of flat-colors similar to these color samples, percentages of the same four basic process colors can be printed in almost endless combinations. But it is very important to remember that while the method for reproducing the four process colors is basically the same for lithography and letterpress printing worldwide, the chemical composition and properties of inks and paper vary somewhat from country to country and even from printer to printer.

In the early 1960's, the idea that quick, effective, and relatively inexpensive architectural embellishment could be obtained through painted surfaces gave rise to brightly colored building exteriors and interiors. Architectural graphics flourished. Today the use of color in architecture and interior design has developed almost exactly parallel to the emergence of postmodernism and ornamentalism. In these two areas color is often either the signal or the confirmation of the designer's intent.

Trendy and fashionable, yes; but these uses of color also set the stage, reinforce the statement, and send the message. The freedom and eclecticism in current fashion derive greater support and vitality from color combinations and variation than from any other influence.

In all of these areas, color doesn't necessarily mean bright color. Enormously satisfying color use and vitality can be found almost anywhere these days: new and renewed buildings, commercial interiors, fashion for any age group, office furniture, and sensitive residential interiors. The most successful color combinations are usually personal and original, muted and subdued. A sense of scale and emphasis applies to color just as it does to size proportion and position in art and music. That is, a small patch of bright color placed next to pale or grayed colors can accentuate their contribution.

The main value of this book is in presenting a large array of color combinations for evaluation and experimentation. Colors are evocative and emotional, and in combinations they can trigger reactions and responses in somewhat the same way letters of the alphabet can combine to spell out messages. There are color combinations here that are absolutely unprecedented by history or tradition, but they work and augment each other in surprising ways. Only individual judgment and preference can determine the most successful and appealing examples. There are enough color examples here to satisfy a passive observer who doesn't need to carry the investigation further, and there certainly is plenty of material to encourage and stimulate additional color innovation.

This book is an invitation to look at color in new ways, to perceive color differently and more acutely, to experiment, and to enjoy.

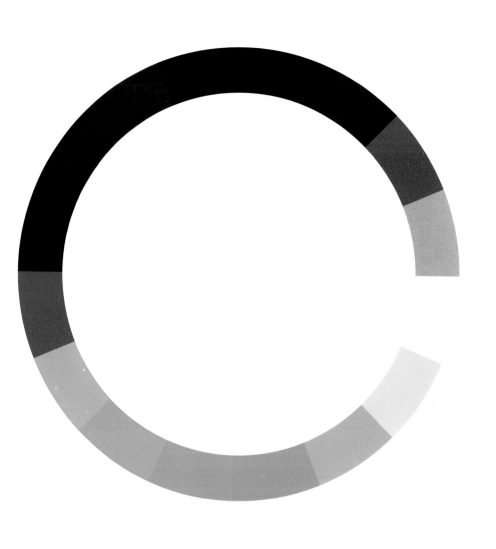

Table of Contents
Two-color combinations

How to use this book
In this book, color schemes that use the same qualities are grouped together, for example, "Bright Clear Colors" (pp14-17) are all bright pastels, but it is also obvious that each combination is somehow different. And speaking of color differences, even though you may be making a multiple color scheme, you'll want to strive for similarities in tone quality in order to achieve an overall harmonious effect.

For color classifications, please refer to the Table of Contents on these first few pages.

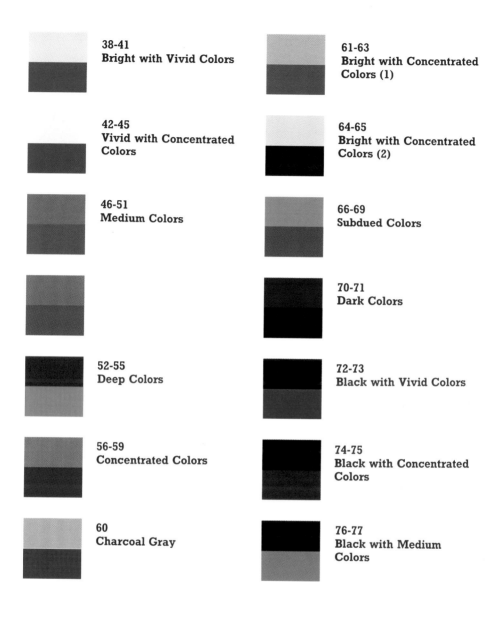

38-41
Bright with Vivid Colors

61-63
Bright with Concentrated Colors (1)

42-45
Vivid with Concentrated Colors

64-65
Bright with Concentrated Colors (2)

46-51
Medium Colors

66-69
Subdued Colors

70-71
Dark Colors

52-55
Deep Colors

72-73
Black with Vivid Colors

56-59
Concentrated Colors

74-75
Black with Concentrated Colors

60
Charcoal Gray

76-77
Black with Medium Colors

Soft tones are first, followed by tones grouped in order of increasing intensity of color. Falling in the middle are the gray color schemes and contrasting color schemes including some unique combinations.

As an exercise, take a sample tone from the book and compare it to those in the Table of Contents, to get a feel for the arrangement of this book.

The essence of the book is to experiment with colors.

Contents

Three-color combinations

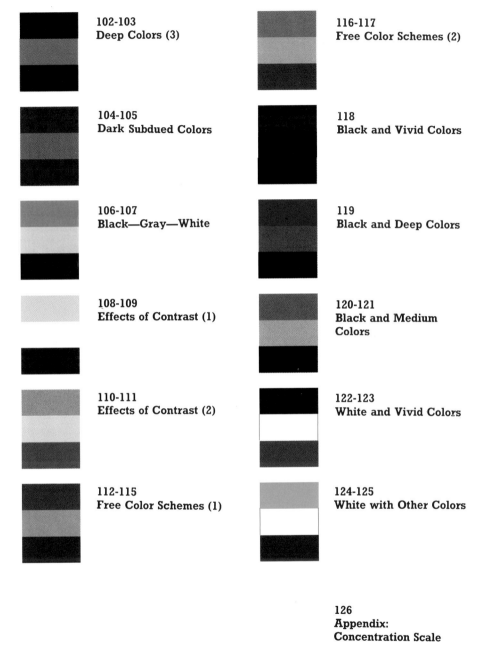

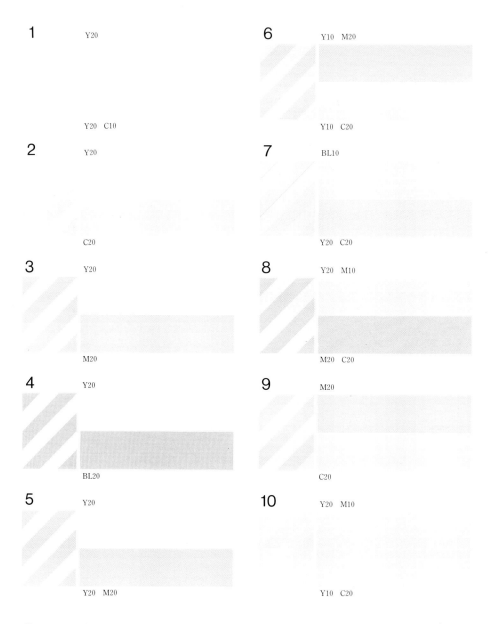

1	Y20		6	Y10 M20
2	Y20 C10		7	Y10 C20
	Y20			BL10
3	C20		8	Y20 C20
	Y20			Y20 M10
4	M20		9	M20 C20
	Y20			M20
5	BL20		10	C20
	Y20			Y20 M10
	Y20 M20			Y10 C20

Very Pale Colors

The differences among the very light colors are subtle and sometimes hard to grasp. However, softer colors are easy to combine: don't worry about colors matching, as long as they convey the same overall message. For instance, in examples 4, 7, and 16 bright gray in combination produces a slightly cool feeling.

6

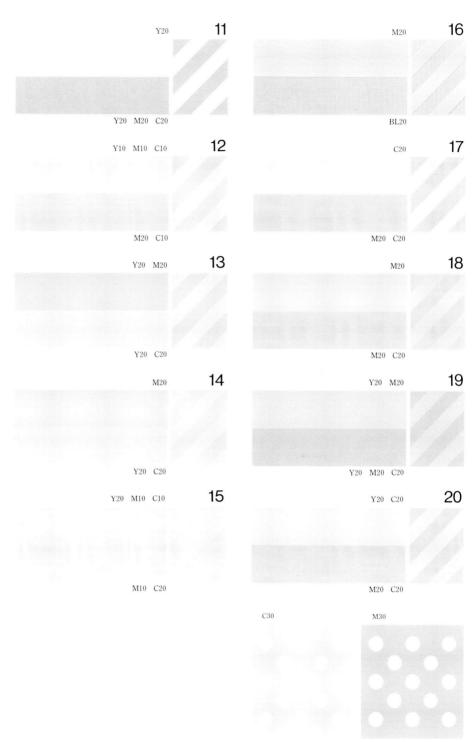

Y20 **11**

Y20 M20 C20

M20 **16**

BL20

Y10 M10 C10 **12**

M20 C10

C20 **17**

M20 C20

Y20 M20 **13**

Y20 C20

M20 **18**

M20 C20

M20 **14**

Y20 C20

Y20 M20 **19**

Y20 M20 C20

Y20 M10 C10 **15**

M10 C20

Y20 C20 **20**

M20 C20

C30

M30

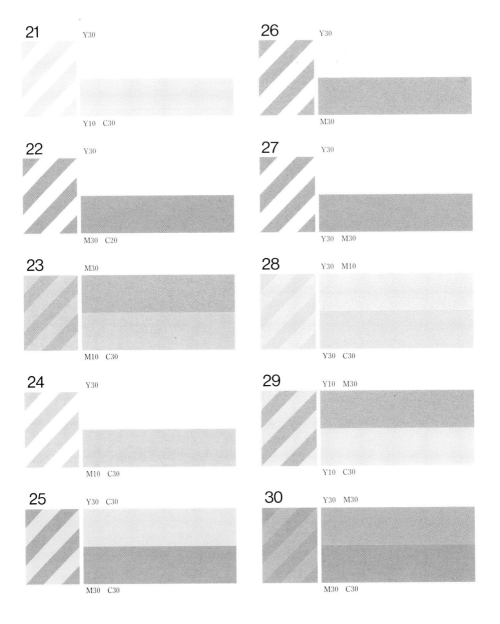

21 Y30
Y10 C30

26 Y30
M30

22 Y30
M30 C20

27 Y30
Y30 M30

23 M30
M10 C30

28 Y30 M10
Y30 C30

24 Y30
M10 C30

29 Y10 M30
Y10 C30

25 Y30 C30
M30 C30

30 Y30 M30
M30 C30

Pale Clear Colors

These light colors have a transparent, cool quality, even though many are from a warm color family. In a dot, stripe, or checkered pattern, the sherbet tones can seem warm, sweet, and sometimes softly sedate.

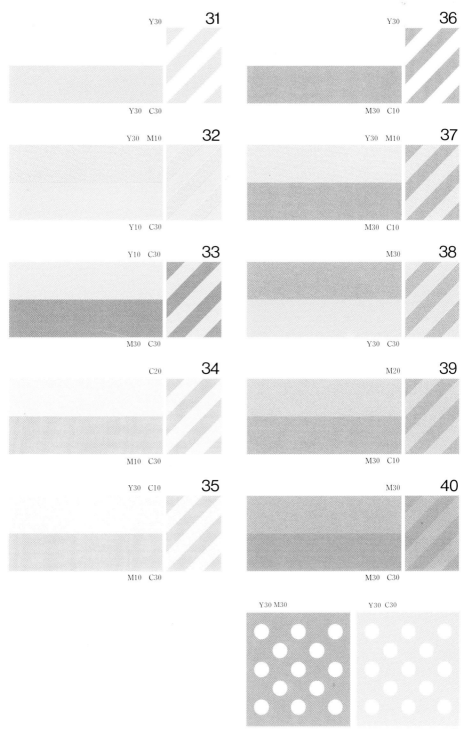

Y30   **31**

Y30   C30

Y30   M10   **32**

Y10   C30

Y10   C30   **33**

M30   C30

C20   **34**

M10   C30

Y30   C10   **35**

M10   C30

Y30   **36**

M30   C10

Y30   M10   **37**

M30   C10

M30   **38**

Y30   C30

M20   **39**

M30   C10

M30   **40**

M30   C30

Y30 M30   Y30 C30

9

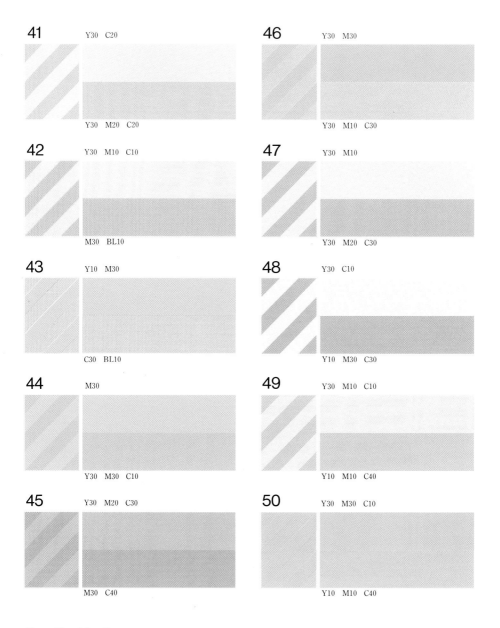

41 Y30 C20

Y30 M20 C20

42 Y30 M10 C10

M30 BL10

43 Y10 M30

C30 BL10

44 M30

Y30 M30 C10

45 Y30 M20 C30

M30 C40

46 Y30 M30

Y30 M10 C30

47 Y30 M10

Y30 M20 C30

48 Y30 C10

Y10 M30 C30

49 Y30 M10 C10

Y10 M10 C40

50 Y30 M30 C10

Y10 M10 C40

Free Combinations

These lighter, duller neutral colors are restful to look at. They may be subdued, but they avoid being melancholy because they contain some degree of brightness.

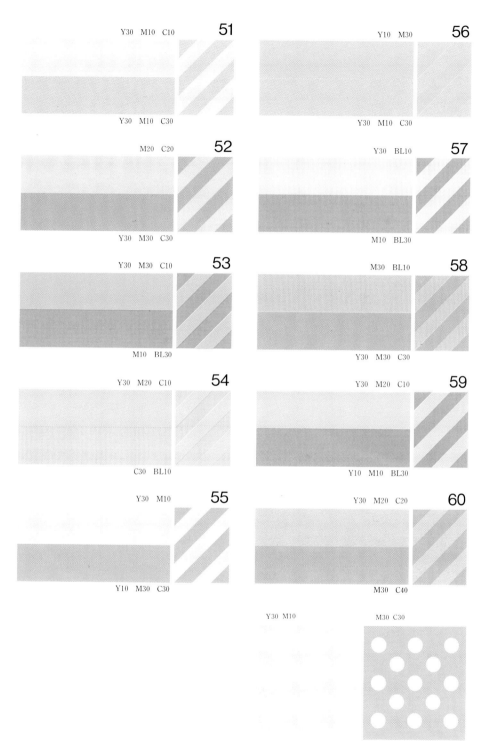

Y30 M10 C10 **51**

Y30 M10 C30

Y10 M30 **56**

Y30 M10 C30

M20 C20 **52**

Y30 M30 C30

Y30 BL10 **57**

M10 BL30

Y30 M30 C10 **53**

M10 BL30

M30 BL10 **58**

Y30 M30 C30

Y30 M20 C10 **54**

C30 BL10

Y30 M20 C10 **59**

Y10 M10 BL30

Y30 M10 **55**

Y10 M30 C30

Y30 M20 C20 **60**

M30 C40

Y30 M10

M30 C30

11

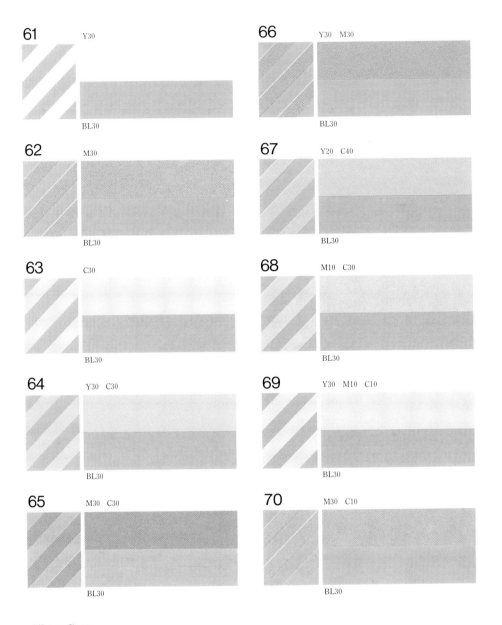

61 Y30

BL30

62 M30

BL30

63 C30

BL30

64 Y30 C30

BL30

65 M30 C30

BL30

66 Y30 M30

BL30

67 Y20 C40

BL30

68 M10 C30

BL30

69 Y30 M10 C10

BL30

70 M30 C10

BL30

Silver Gray
The addition of silver gray creates cool,
elegant, pretty combinations. In Japan,
these are typical spring color schemes.
For greater contrast, try darker gray.

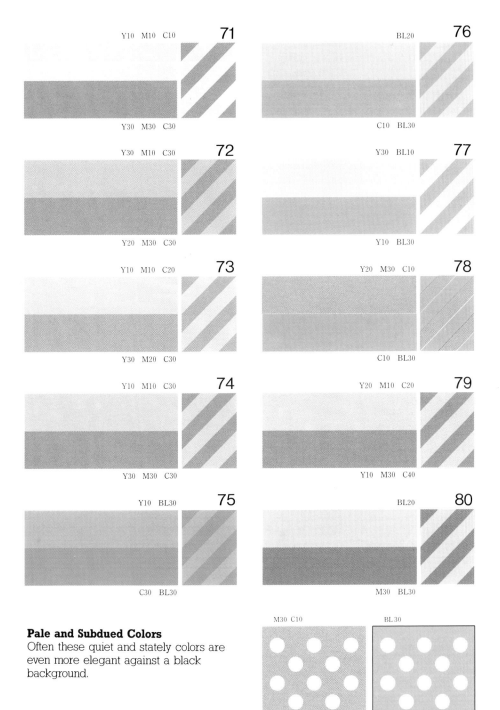

Y10 M10 C10 **71**

Y30 M30 C30

BL20 **76**

C10 BL30

Y30 M10 C30 **72**

Y20 M30 C30

Y30 BL10 **77**

Y10 BL30

Y10 M10 C20 **73**

Y30 M20 C30

Y20 M30 C10 **78**

C10 BL30

Y10 M10 C30 **74**

Y30 M30 C30

Y20 M10 C20 **79**

Y10 M30 C40

Y10 BL30 **75**

C30 BL30

BL20 **80**

M30 BL30

Pale and Subdued Colors
Often these quiet and stately colors are even more elegant against a black background.

M30 C10

BL 30

13

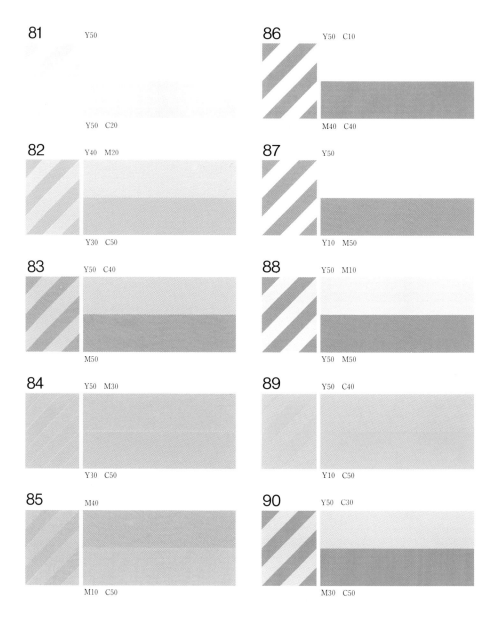

81	Y50	86	Y50 C10
	Y50 C20		M40 C40
82	Y40 M20	87	Y50
	Y30 C50		Y10 M50
83	Y50 C40	88	Y50 M10
	M50		Y50 M50
84	Y50 M30	89	Y50 C40
	Y30 C50		Y10 C50
85	M40	90	Y50 C30
	M10 C50		M30 C50

Bright Clear Colors

These bright and healthy colors have a degree of brilliance. This grouping also has a powdery quality. Think of them as young colors for spring casual wear, for romantic storybook pictures, or for evoking a tropical feeling.

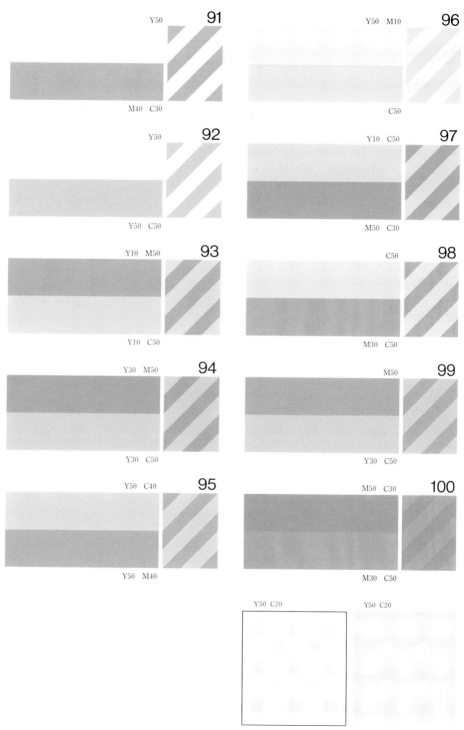

Y50   **91**

M40   C30

Y50   M10   **96**

C50

Y50   **92**

Y50   C50

Y10   C50   **97**

M50   C30

Y10   M50   **93**

Y10   C50

C50   **98**

M30   C50

Y30   M50   **94**

Y30   C50

M50   **99**

Y30   C50

Y50   C40   **95**

Y50   M40

M50   C30   **100**

M30   C50

Y50   C20

Y50   C20

15

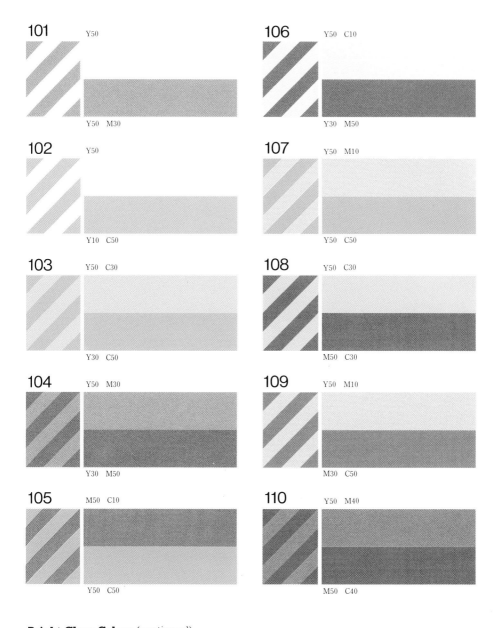

101   Y50

Y50   M30

102   Y50

Y10   C50

103   Y50   C30

Y30   C50

104   Y50   M30

Y30   M50

105   M50   C10

Y50   C50

106   Y50   C10

Y30   M50

107   Y50   M10

Y50   C50

108   Y50   C30

M50   C30

109   Y50   M10

M30   C50

110   Y50   M40

M50   C40

Bright Clear Colors (continued)

16

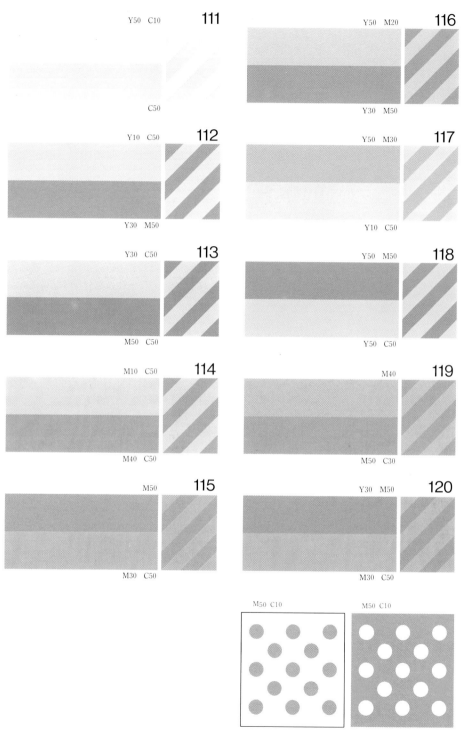

Y50 C10 **111**

C50

Y50 M20 **116**

Y30 M50

Y10 C50 **112**

Y30 M50

Y50 M30 **117**

Y10 C50

Y30 C50 **113**

M50 C50

Y50 M50 **118**

Y50 C50

M10 C50 **114**

M40 C50

M40 **119**

M50 C30

M50 **115**

M30 C50

Y30 M50 **120**

M30 C50

M50 C10

M50 C10

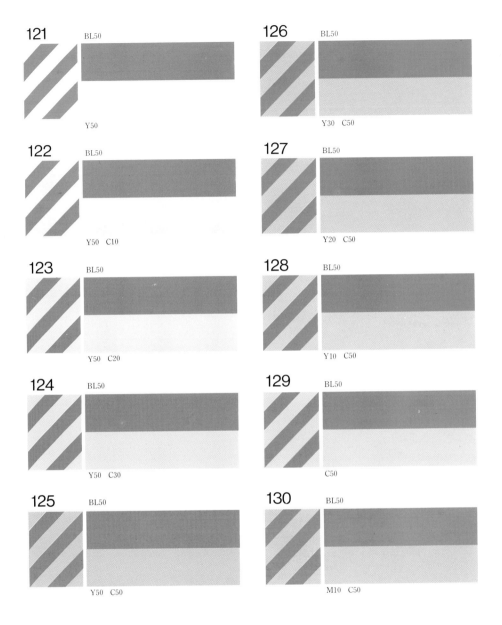

121 BL50 / Y50	**126** BL50 / Y30 C50
122 BL50 / Y50 C10	**127** BL50 / Y20 C50
123 BL50 / Y50 C20	**128** BL50 / Y10 C50
124 BL50 / Y50 C30	**129** BL50 / C50
125 BL50 / Y50 C50	**130** BL50 / M10 C50

Medium Grays

Use gray as an accent as well as a principal color. Medium gray is especially good for enhancing other colors (if you aren't sure what color to use, try gray first). The colors and gray on these pages contain the same degree of brightness, and the resulting combinations achieve a balance between quiet gray and bright color.

18

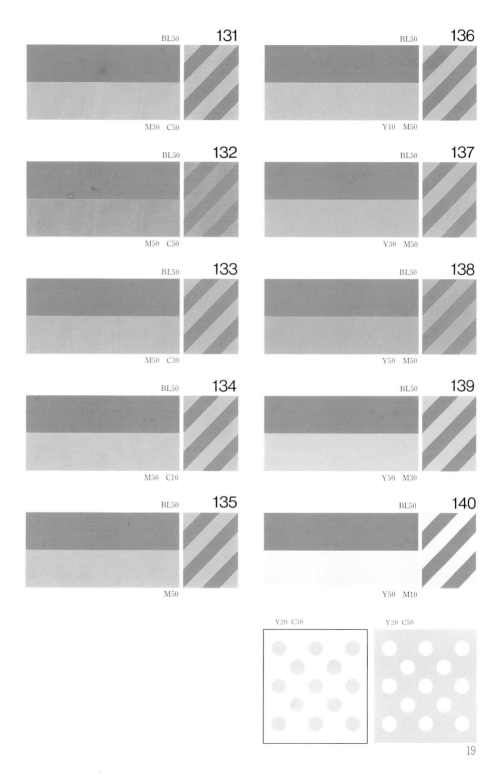

BL50 **131**
M30 C50

BL50 **136**
Y10 M50

BL50 **132**
M50 C50

BL50 **137**
Y30 M50

BL50 **133**
M50 C30

BL50 **138**
Y50 M50

BL50 **134**
M50 C10

BL50 **139**
Y50 M30

BL50 **135**
M50

BL50 **140**
Y50 M10

Y20 C50

Y20 C50

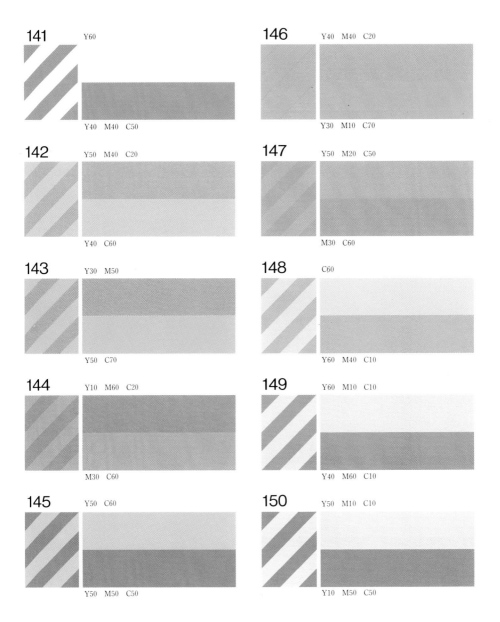

141 Y60

Y40 M40 C50

146 Y40 M40 C20

Y30 M10 C70

142 Y50 M40 C20

Y40 C60

147 Y50 M20 C50

M30 C60

143 Y30 M50

Y50 C70

148 C60

Y60 M40 C10

144 Y10 M60 C20

M30 C60

149 Y60 M10 C10

Y40 M60 C10

145 Y50 C60

Y50 M50 C50

150 Y50 M10 C10

Y10 M50 C50

Free Combinations of Bright Colors
These color combinations have a broad
range of applications, from interior design
to fashion. Bright colors are placed next
to dull colors, but each has enough
brightness to make the mix lively.

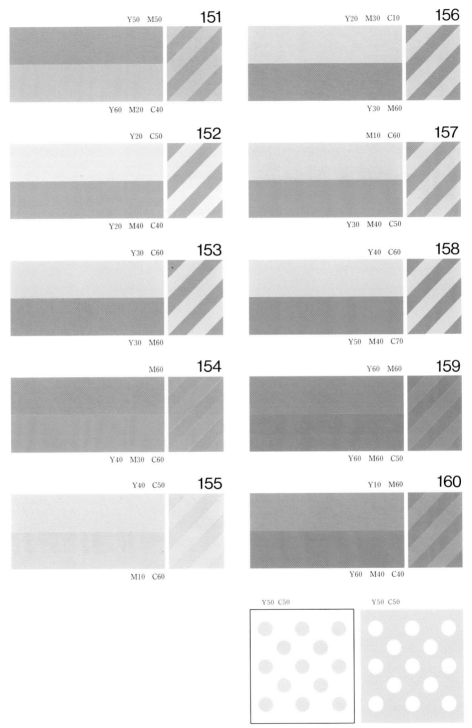

Y50　M50　**151**

Y60　M20　C40

Y20　C50　**152**

Y20　M40　C40

Y30　C60　**153**

Y30　M60

M60　**154**

Y40　M30　C60

Y40　C50　**155**

M10　C60

Y20　M30　C10　**156**

Y30　M60

M10　C60　**157**

Y30　M40　C50

Y40　C60　**158**

Y50　M40　C70

Y60　M60　**159**

Y60　M60　C50

Y10　M60　**160**

Y60　M40　C40

Y50　C50

Y50　C50

21

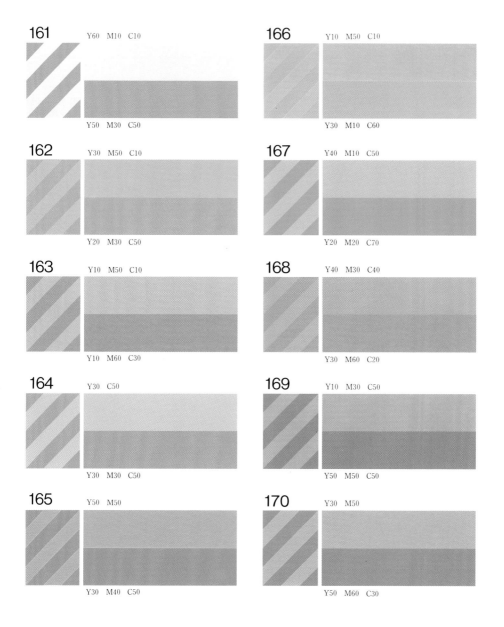

161 Y60 M10 C10
Y50 M30 C50

166 Y10 M50 C10
Y30 M10 C60

162 Y30 M50 C10
Y20 M30 C50

167 Y40 M10 C50
Y20 M20 C70

163 Y10 M50 C10
Y10 M60 C30

168 Y40 M30 C40
Y30 M60 C20

164 Y30 C50
Y30 M30 C50

169 Y10 M30 C50
Y50 M50 C50

165 Y50 M50
Y30 M40 C50

170 Y30 M50
Y50 M60 C30

Free Combinations of Bright Colors
(continued)

22

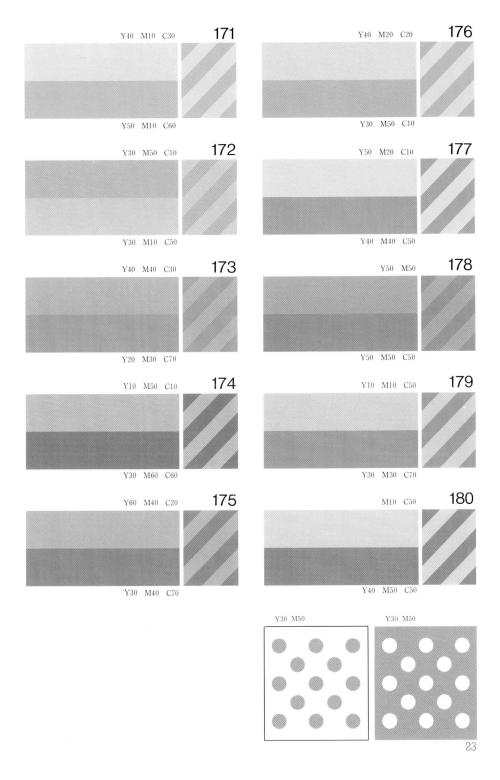

Y40 M10 C30 **171**

Y50 M10 C60

Y40 M20 C20 **176**

Y30 M50 C10

Y30 M50 C10 **172**

Y30 M10 C50

Y50 M20 C10 **177**

Y40 M40 C50

Y40 M40 C30 **173**

Y20 M30 C70

Y50 M50 **178**

Y50 M50 C50

Y10 M50 C10 **174**

Y30 M60 C60

Y10 M10 C50 **179**

Y30 M30 C70

Y60 M40 C20 **175**

Y30 M40 C70

M10 C50 **180**

Y40 M50 C50

Y30 M50

Y30 M50

23

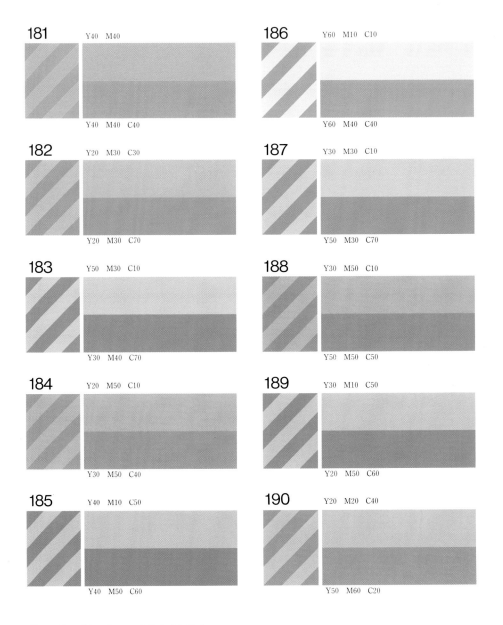

181 Y40 M40

Y40 M40 C40

186 Y60 M10 C10

Y60 M40 C40

182 Y20 M30 C30

Y20 M30 C70

187 Y30 M30 C10

Y50 M30 C70

183 Y50 M30 C10

Y30 M40 C70

188 Y30 M50 C10

Y50 M50 C50

184 Y20 M50 C10

Y30 M50 C40

189 Y30 M10 C50

Y20 M50 C60

185 Y40 M10 C50

Y40 M50 C60

190 Y20 M20 C40

Y50 M60 C20

Free Combinations of Bright Colors
(continued)

24

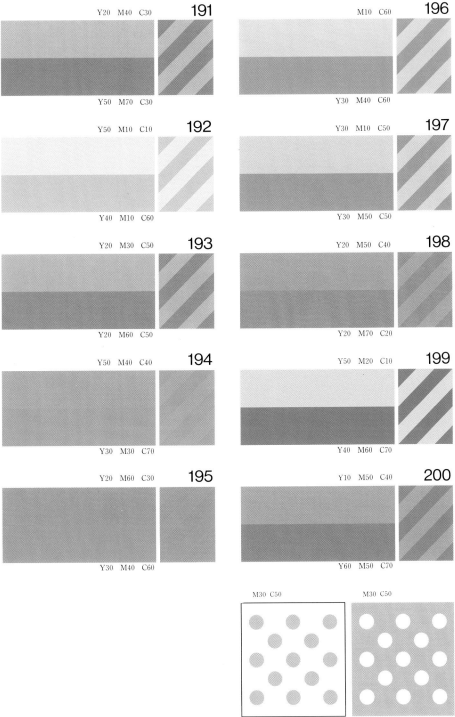

191   Y20 M40 C30 / Y50 M70 C30

192   Y50 M10 C10 / Y40 M10 C60

193   Y20 M30 C50 / Y20 M60 C50

194   Y50 M40 C40 / Y30 M30 C70

195   Y20 M60 C30 / Y30 M40 C60

196   M10 C60 / Y30 M40 C60

197   Y30 M10 C50 / Y30 M50 C50

198   Y20 M50 C40 / Y20 M70 C20

199   Y50 M20 C10 / Y40 M60 C70

200   Y10 M50 C40 / Y60 M50 C70

M30 C50

M30 C50

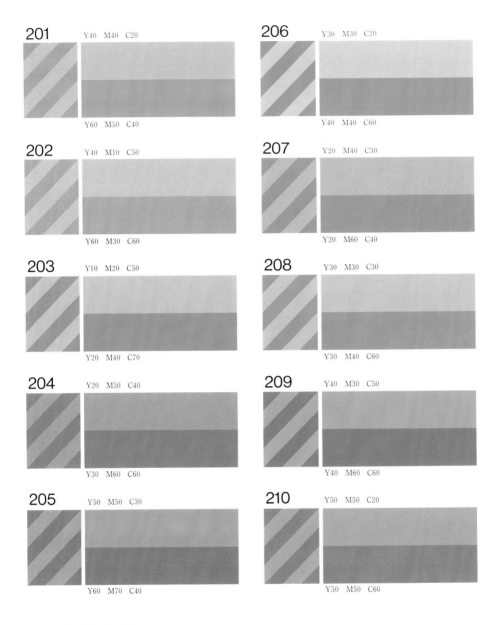

| 201 | Y40 M40 C20 | | 206 | Y30 M30 C20 |
| Y60 M50 C40 | | | Y40 M40 C60 | |

| 202 | Y40 M10 C50 | | 207 | Y20 M40 C30 |
| Y60 M30 C60 | | | Y20 M60 C40 | |

| 203 | Y10 M20 C50 | | 208 | Y30 M30 C30 |
| Y20 M40 C70 | | | Y30 M40 C60 | |

| 204 | Y20 M50 C40 | | 209 | Y40 M30 C50 |
| Y30 M60 C60 | | | Y40 M60 C60 | |

| 205 | Y50 M50 C30 | | 210 | Y50 M50 C20 |
| Y60 M70 C40 | | | Y50 M50 C60 | |

Bright Subdued Colors

Even though colors may be subdued, they can still contrast. (To remove the color contrast completely, choose analogous colors of the same intensity.)

Combining bright and subdued colors is a challenge. It is important to consider the characteristics, personality, and possible emotional context of each color. Exam-

ples 201 through 205 pair colors within the same family, while examples 211 through 220 show subdued colors from different families—very effective in the right setting.

26

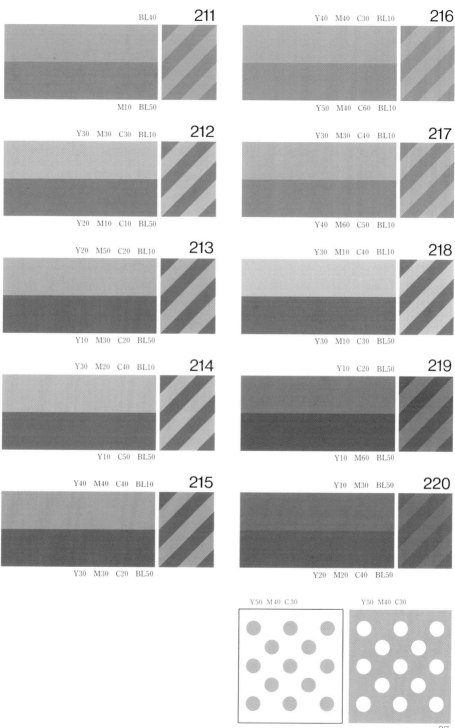

BL40 **211**

M10   BL50

Y40   M40   C30   BL10 **216**

Y50   M40   C60   BL10

Y30   M30   C30   BL10 **212**

Y20   M10   C10   BL50

Y30   M30   C40   BL10 **217**

Y40   M60   C50   BL10

Y20   M50   C20   BL10 **213**

Y10   M30   C20   BL50

Y30   M10   C40   BL10 **218**

Y30   M10   C30   BL50

Y30   M20   C40   BL10 **214**

Y10   C50   BL50

Y10   C20   BL50 **219**

Y10   M60   BL50

Y40   M40   C40   BL10 **215**

Y30   M30   C20   BL50

Y10   M30   BL50 **220**

Y20   M20   C40   BL50

Y50   M40   C30   Y50   M40   C30

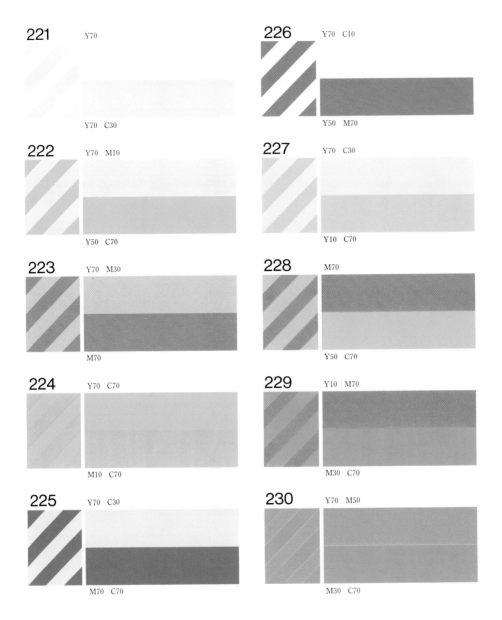

221 Y70

Y70 C30

222 Y70 M10

Y50 C70

223 Y70 M30

M70

224 Y70 C70

M10 C70

225 Y70 C30

M70 C70

226 Y70 C10

Y50 M70

227 Y70 C30

Y10 C70

228 M70

Y50 C70

229 Y10 M70

M30 C70

230 Y70 M50

M30 C70

Vivid and Bright Colors
Visions of fresh fruit spring to mind with these bright and light-hearted pastels. These are young, tropical color schemes; in fashion they might be used for casual spring and summer wear.

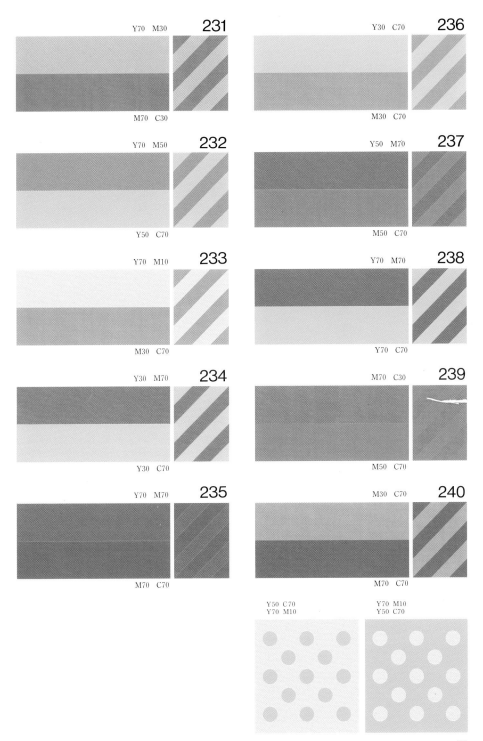

231 Y70 M30
M70 C30

236 Y30 C70
M30 C70

232 Y70 M50
Y50 C70

237 Y50 M70
M50 C70

233 Y70 M10
M30 C70

238 Y70 M70
Y70 C70

234 Y30 M70
Y30 C70

239 M70 C30
M50 C70

235 Y70 M70
M70 C70

240 M30 C70
M70 C70

Y50 C70
Y70 M10

Y70 M10
Y50 C70

29

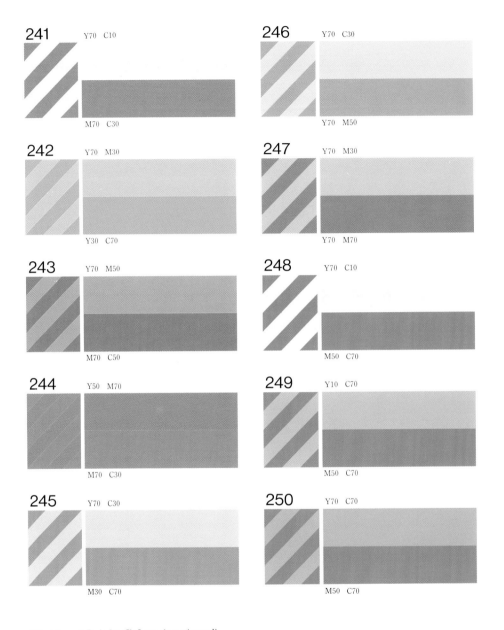

241   Y70   C10

M70   C30

242   Y70   M30

Y30   C70

243   Y70   M50

M70   C50

244   Y50   M70

M70   C30

245   Y70   C30

M30   C70

246   Y70   C30

Y70   M50

247   Y70   M30

Y70   M70

248   Y70   C10

M50   C70

249   Y10   C70

M50   C70

250   Y70   C70

M50   C70

Vivid and Bright Colors (continued)

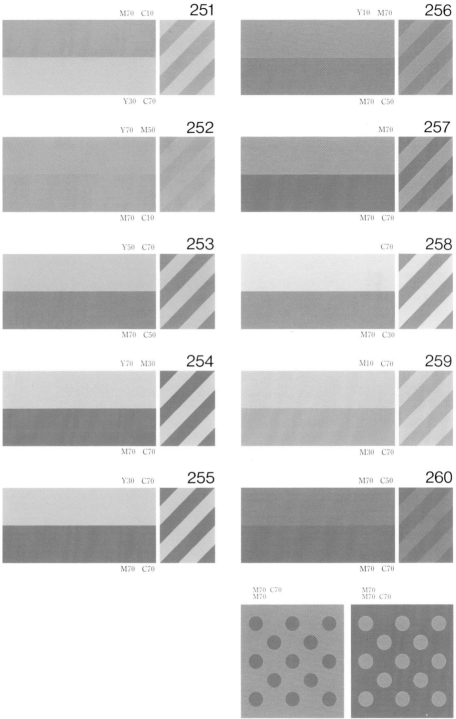

M70 C10 **251**

Y30 C70

Y10 M70 **256**

M70 C50

Y70 M50 **252**

M70 C10

M70 **257**

M70 C70

Y50 C70 **253**

M70 C50

C70 **258**

M70 C30

Y70 M30 **254**

M70 C70

M10 C70 **259**

M30 C70

Y30 C70 **255**

M70 C70

M70 C50 **260**

M70 C70

M70 C70
M70

M70
M70 C70

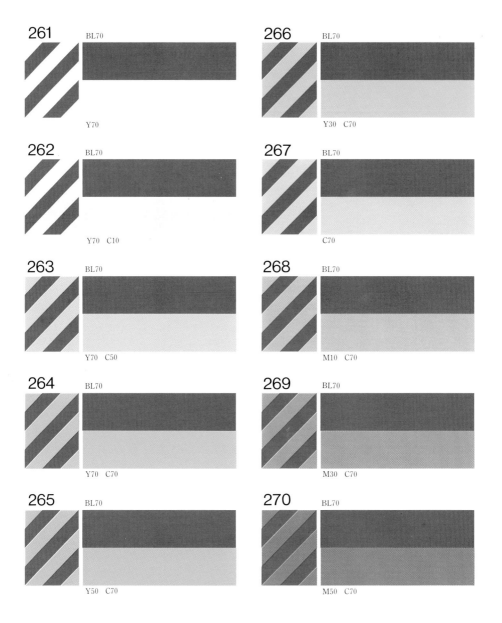

261 BL70 / Y70

262 BL70 / Y70 C10

263 BL70 / Y70 C50

264 BL70 / Y70 C70

265 BL70 / Y50 C70

266 BL70 / Y30 C70

267 BL70 / C70

268 BL70 / M10 C70

269 BL70 / M30 C70

270 BL70 / M50 C70

Slate Gray

Slate gray is between medium and charcoal gray. Technically, gray is considered to be colorless (like black or white); but in terms of color schemes, it falls in the blue family, especially the dark and near-black grays. Matched here with either related cool colors or contrasting with warm colors, slate gray produces startling effects.

If cloth is dyed gray, it turns either slightly reddish or bluish. For a purer gray color, cotton or wool is usuallly first bleached white or dyed black—a process called *topping*—then made into various shades of gray by adding a mixture of black and white.

32

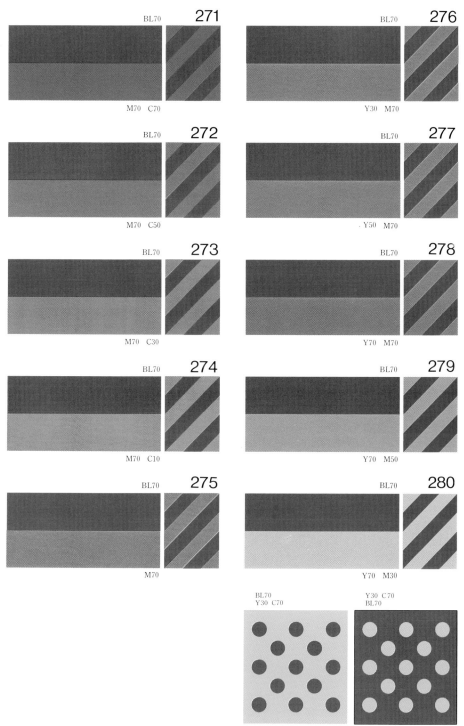

BL70 **271**

M70 C70

BL70 **276**

Y30 M70

BL70 **272**

M70 C50

BL70 **277**

Y50 M70

BL70 **273**

M70 C30

BL70 **278**

Y70 M70

BL70 **274**

M70 C10

BL70 **279**

Y70 M50

BL70 **275**

M70

BL70 **280**

Y70 M30

BL70
Y30 C70

Y30 C70
BL70

33

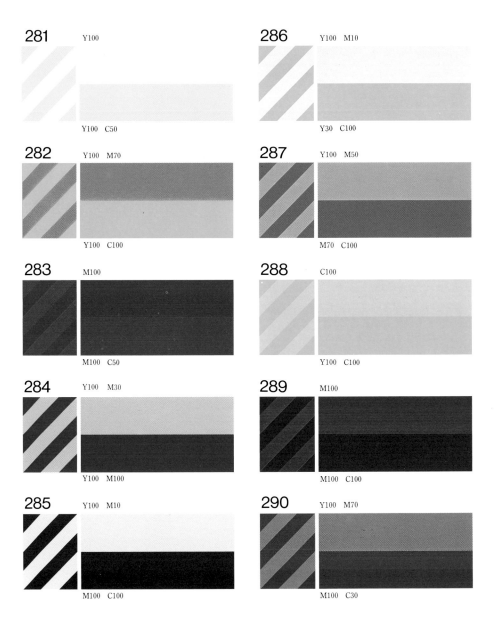

281 Y100
Y100 C50

286 Y100 M10
Y30 C100

282 Y100 M70
Y100 C100

287 Y100 M50
M70 C100

283 M100
M100 C50

288 C100
Y100 C100

284 Y100 M30
Y100 M100

289 M100
M100 C100

285 Y100 M10
M100 C100

290 Y100 M70
M100 C30

Vivid Colors

These color schemes use strong primary colors that broadcast a very clear message. Each color has very distinct characteristics, and reactions to these combinations are more specific than they are to subtle colors. The combinations here suggest heat, health, vitality, aggressiveness, humor, fun, sporting events, citrus flavors, 34

and some current high fashion. Their charm lies in boldness and beauty, so use them in big, dramatic ways.

Color brilliance is relative to the medium used: 100% colors look far more brilliant in printing than they do in paints or dyes, and the same color can look quite different if printed on silk or cotton.

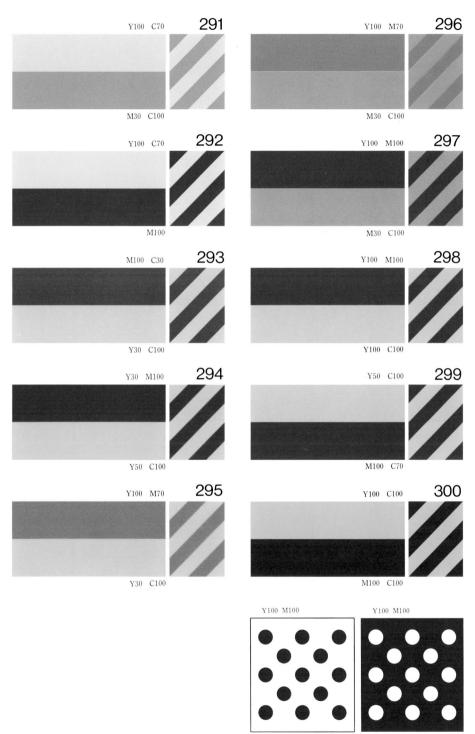

Y100 C70 **291**

M30 C100

Y100 M70 **296**

M30 C100

Y100 C70 **292**

M100

Y100 M100 **297**

M30 C100

M100 C30 **293**

Y30 C100

Y100 M100 **298**

Y100 C100

Y30 M100 **294**

Y50 C100

Y50 C100 **299**

M100 C70

Y100 M70 **295**

Y30 C100

Y100 C100 **300**

M100 C100

Y100 M100

Y100 M100

35

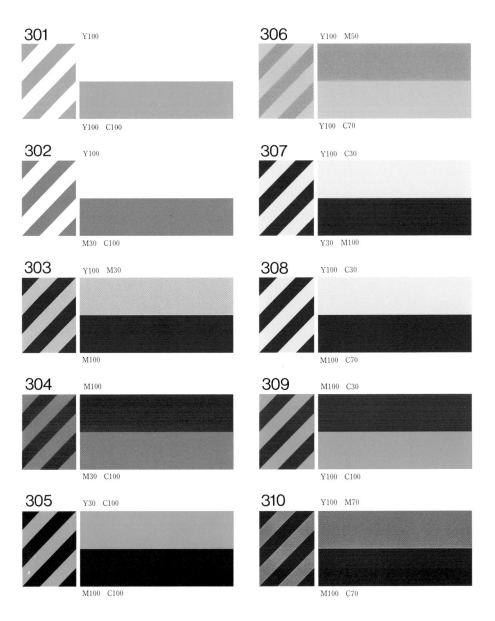

301 Y100

Y100 C100

302 Y100

M30 C100

303 Y100 M30

M100

304 M100

M30 C100

305 Y30 C100

M100 C100

306 Y100 M50

Y100 C70

307 Y100 C30

Y30 M100

308 Y100 C30

M100 C70

309 M100 C30

Y100 C100

310 Y100 M70

M100 C70

Vivid Colors (continued)

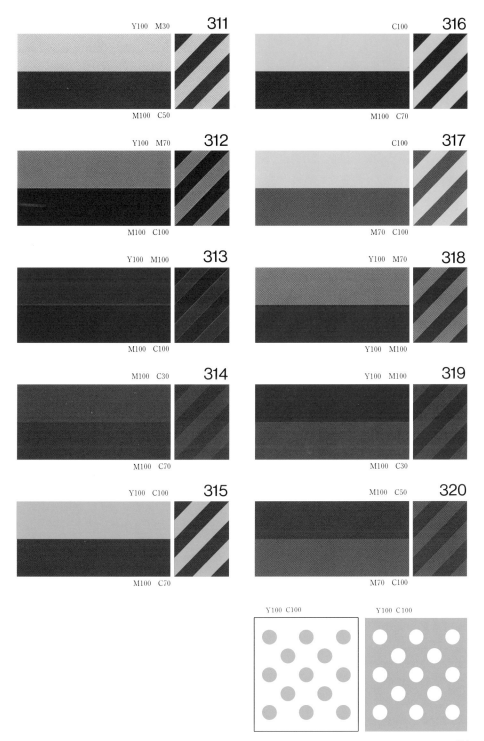

Y100 M30 **311**

M100 C50

C100 **316**

M100 C70

Y100 M70 **312**

M100 C100

C100 **317**

M70 C100

Y100 M100 **313**

M100 C100

Y100 M70 **318**

Y100 M100

M100 C30 **314**

M100 C70

Y100 M100 **319**

M100 C30

Y100 C100 **315**

M100 C70

M100 C50 **320**

M70 C100

Y100 C100

Y100 C100

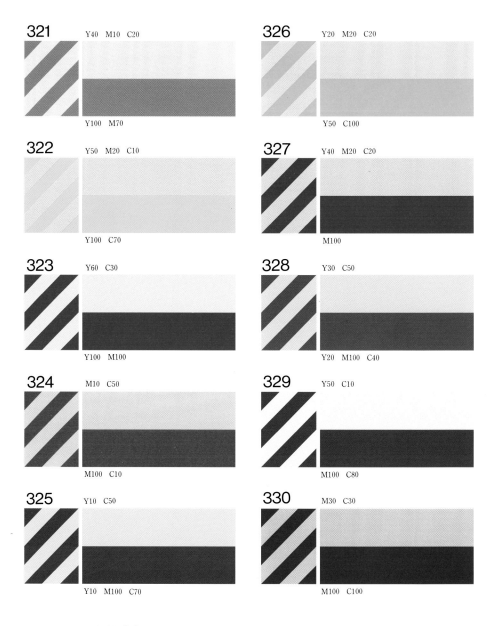

321   Y40   M10   C20
Y100   M70

326   Y20   M20   C20
Y50   C100

322   Y50   M20   C10
Y100   C70

327   Y40   M20   C20
M100

323   Y60   C30
Y100   M100

328   Y30   C50
Y20   M100   C40

324   M10   C50
M100   C10

329   Y50   C10
M100   C80

325   Y10   C50
Y10   M100   C70

330   M30   C30
M100   C100

Bright with Vivid Colors

These contrasting color schemes use colors with very similar levels of brightness and brilliance. Some have gorgeous effects, some seem sweet or frivolous. They are best used as highlights in a multicolor pattern, such as in a formal Japanese kimono. In using them, think more about the overall impression than whether the colors do well together. For instance, in Japanese classical drama (Kubuki), the colors in example 323 are sometimes used for the costume of young girls (and, at the same time, the city of Tokyo uses example 331 for its buses).

38

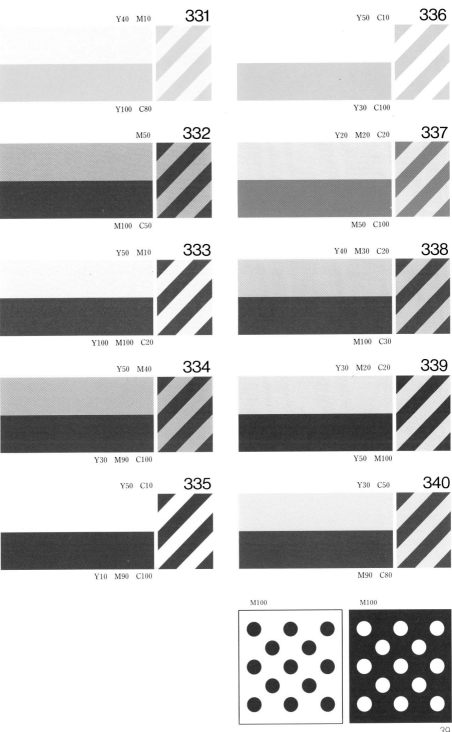

Y40 M10 **331**
Y100 C80

Y50 C10 **336**
Y30 C100

M50 **332**
M100 C50

Y20 M20 C20 **337**
M50 C100

Y50 M10 **333**
Y100 M100 C20

Y40 M30 C20 **338**
M100 C30

Y50 M40 **334**
Y30 M90 C100

Y30 M20 C20 **339**
Y50 M100

Y50 C10 **335**
Y10 M90 C100

Y30 C50 **340**
M90 C80

M100

M100

39

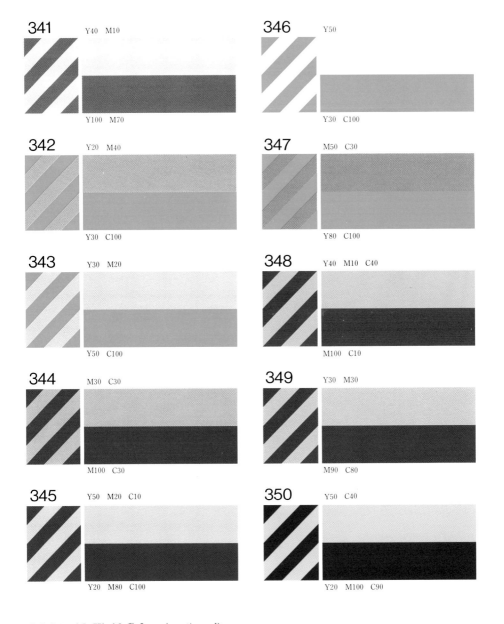

341 Y40 M10

Y100 M70

346 Y50

Y30 C100

342 Y20 M40

Y30 C100

347 M50 C30

Y80 C100

343 Y30 M20

Y50 C100

348 Y40 M10 C40

M100 C10

344 M30 C30

M100 C30

349 Y30 M30

M90 C80

345 Y50 M20 C10

Y20 M80 C100

350 Y50 C40

Y20 M100 C90

Bright with Vivid Colors (continued)

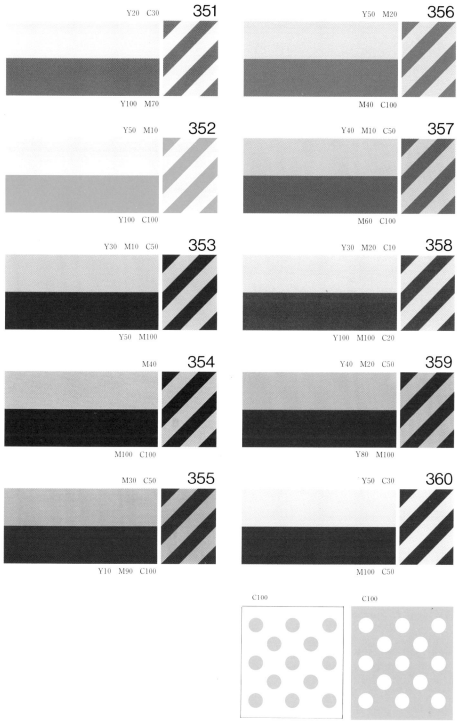

Y20 C30 **351**
Y100 M70

Y50 M10 **352**
Y100 C100

Y30 M10 C50 **353**
Y50 M100

M40 **354**
M100 C100

M30 C50 **355**
Y10 M90 C100

Y50 M20 **356**
M40 C100

Y40 M10 C50 **357**
M60 C100

Y30 M20 C10 **358**
Y100 M100 C20

Y40 M20 C50 **359**
Y80 M100

Y50 C30 **360**
M100 C50

C100

C100

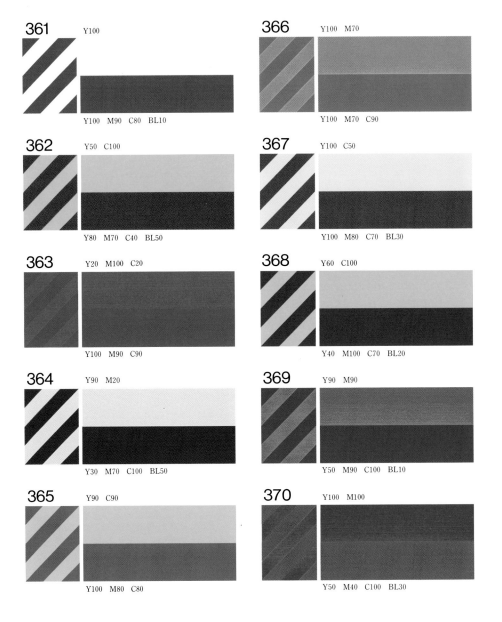

361 Y100

Y100 M90 C80 BL10

362 Y50 C100

Y80 M70 C40 BL50

363 Y20 M100 C20

Y100 M90 C90

364 Y90 M20

Y30 M70 C100 BL50

365 Y90 C90

Y100 M80 C80

366 Y100 M70

Y100 M70 C90

367 Y100 C50

Y100 M80 C70 BL30

368 Y60 C100

Y40 M100 C70 BL20

369 Y90 M90

Y50 M90 C100 BL10

370 Y100 M100

Y50 M40 C100 BL30

Vivid with Concentrated Colors

At either side of the color wheel, the differences among colors become increasingly fine. Darker colors tend to be among the browns, purples, blues, greens, and grays. Pairing a dark color with a brilliant color serves to emphasize the brilliant color as well as the contrast.

These color schemes are comparatively easy to arrange and make a strong graphic statement.

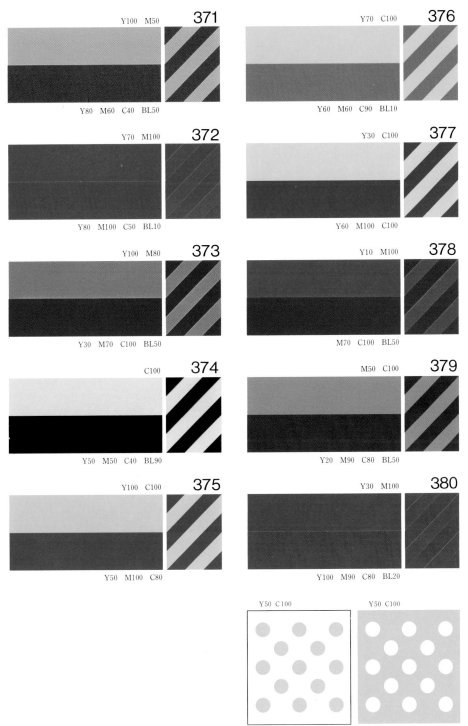

Y100 M50 **371**

Y80 M60 C40 BL50

Y70 M100 **372**

Y80 M100 C50 BL10

Y100 M80 **373**

Y30 M70 C100 BL50

C100 **374**

Y50 M50 C40 BL90

Y100 C100 **375**

Y50 M100 C80

Y70 C100 **376**

Y60 M60 C90 BL10

Y30 C100 **377**

Y60 M100 C100

Y10 M100 **378**

M70 C100 BL50

M50 C100 **379**

Y20 M90 C80 BL50

Y30 M100 **380**

Y100 M90 C80 BL20

Y50 C100

Y50 C100

43

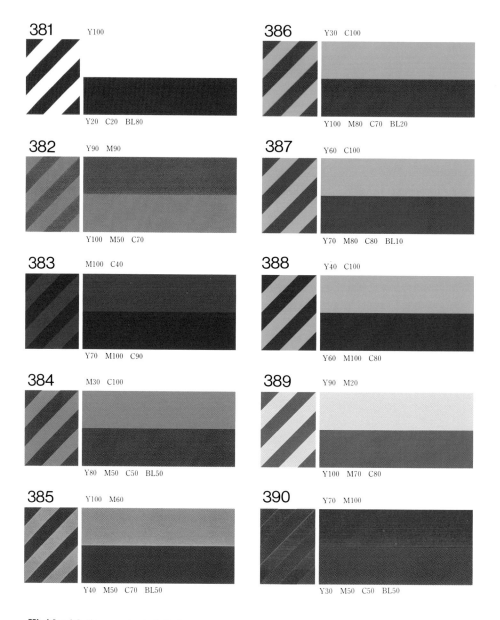

381 Y100

Y20 C20 BL80

386 Y30 C100

Y100 M80 C70 BL20

382 Y90 M90

Y100 M50 C70

387 Y60 C100

Y70 M80 C80 BL10

383 M100 C40

Y70 M100 C90

388 Y40 C100

Y60 M100 C80

384 M30 C100

Y80 M50 C50 BL50

389 Y90 M20

Y100 M70 C80

385 Y100 M60

Y40 M50 C70 BL50

390 Y70 M100

Y30 M50 C50 BL50

Vivid with Concentrated Colors
(continued)

44

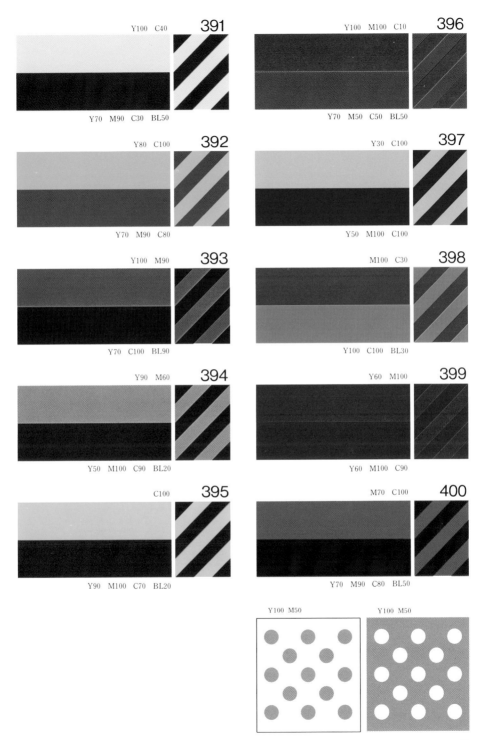

Y100 C40 **391**

Y70 M90 C30 BL50

Y100 M100 C10 **396**

Y70 M50 C50 BL50

Y80 C100 **392**

Y70 M90 C80

Y30 C100 **397**

Y50 M100 C100

Y100 M90 **393**

Y70 C100 BL90

M100 C30 **398**

Y100 C100 BL30

Y90 M60 **394**

Y50 M100 C90 BL20

Y60 M100 **399**

Y60 M100 C90

C100 **395**

Y90 M100 C70 BL20

M70 C100 **400**

Y70 M90 C80 BL50

Y100 M50

Y100 M50

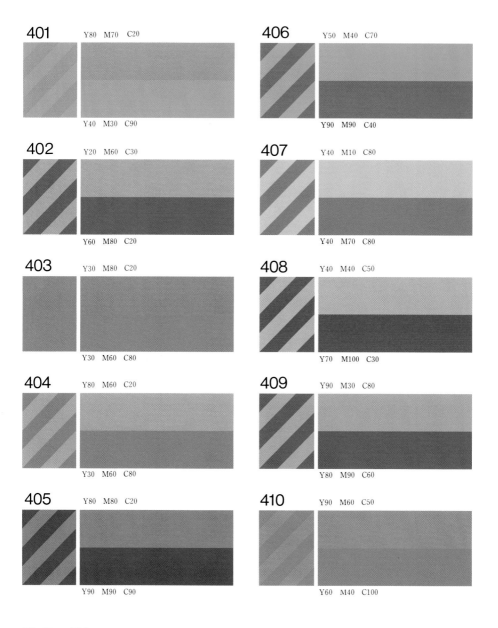

401 Y80 M70 C20
Y40 M30 C90

406 Y50 M40 C70
Y90 M90 C40

402 Y20 M60 C30
Y60 M80 C20

407 Y40 M10 C80
Y40 M70 C80

403 Y30 M80 C20
Y30 M60 C80

408 Y40 M40 C50
Y70 M100 C30

404 Y80 M60 C20
Y30 M60 C80

409 Y90 M30 C80
Y80 M90 C60

405 Y80 M80 C20
Y90 M90 C90

410 Y90 M60 C50
Y60 M40 C100

Medium Colors

Randomly selected, these slightly dull colors are combined with brighter, more intense colors for traditional effect and crispness. In example 401, a red–blue color scheme, you could easily substitute a brown for the burnt orange.

These colors can evoke moods, sounds, memories, eras, and seasons just as powerfully and immediately as brighter colors.

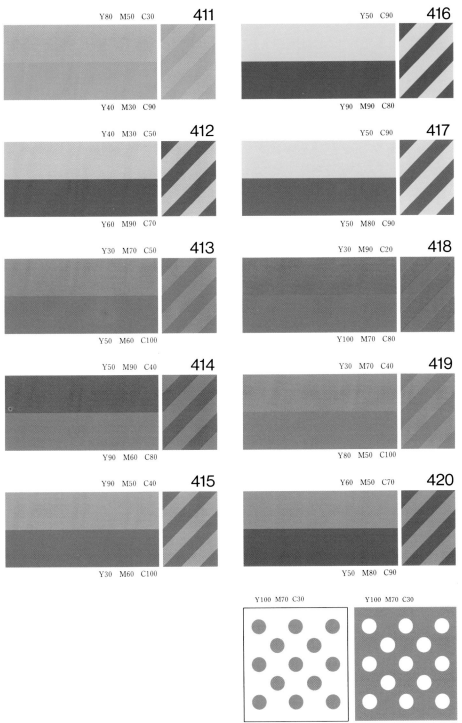

Y80 M50 C30 **411**

Y40 M30 C90

Y40 M30 C50 **412**

Y60 M90 C70

Y30 M70 C50 **413**

Y50 M60 C100

Y50 M90 C40 **414**

Y90 M60 C80

Y90 M50 C40 **415**

Y30 M60 C100

Y50 C90 **416**

Y90 M90 C80

Y50 C90 **417**

Y50 M80 C90

Y30 M90 C20 **418**

Y100 M70 C80

Y30 M70 C40 **419**

Y80 M50 C100

Y60 M50 C70 **420**

Y50 M80 C90

Y100 M70 C30   Y100 M70 C30

47

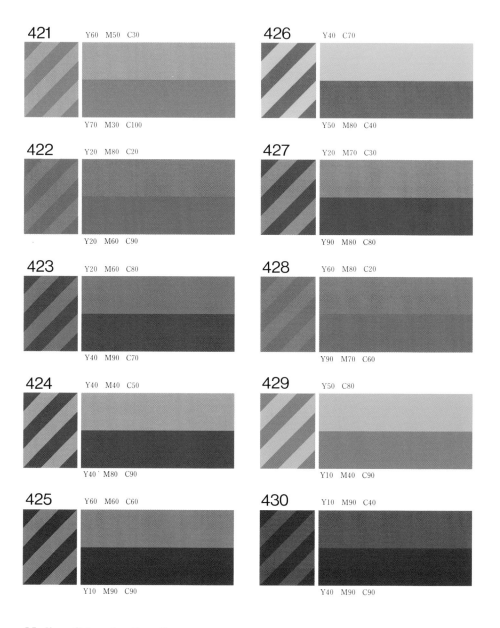

421   Y60   M50   C30

Y70   M30   C100

422   Y20   M80   C20

Y20   M60   C90

423   Y20   M60   C80

Y40   M90   C70

424   Y40   M40   C50

Y40   M80   C90

425   Y60   M60   C60

Y10   M90   C90

426   Y40   C70

Y50   M80   C40

427   Y20   M70   C30

Y90   M80   C80

428   Y60   M80   C20

Y90   M70   C60

429   Y50   C80

Y10   M40   C90

430   Y10   M90   C40

Y40   M90   C90

Medium Colors (continued)

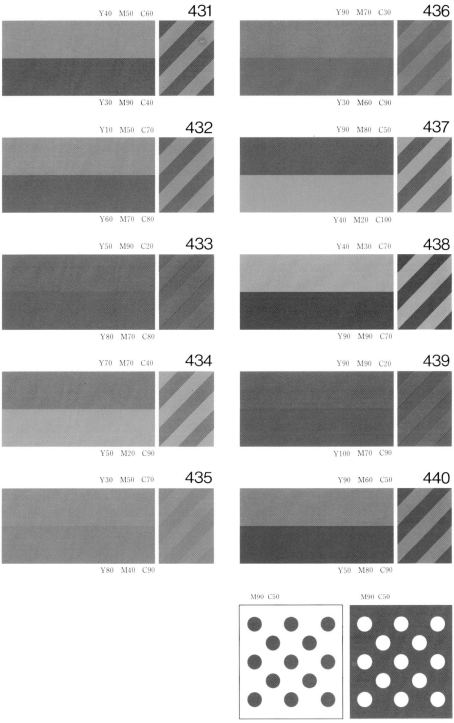

Y40 M50 C60 **431**
Y30 M90 C40

Y90 M70 C30 **436**
Y30 M60 C90

Y10 M50 C70 **432**
Y60 M70 C80

Y90 M80 C50 **437**
Y40 M20 C100

Y50 M90 C20 **433**
Y80 M70 C80

Y40 M30 C70 **438**
Y90 M90 C70

Y70 M70 C40 **434**
Y50 M20 C90

Y90 M90 C20 **439**
Y100 M70 C90

Y30 M50 C70 **435**
Y80 M40 C90

Y90 M60 C50 **440**
Y50 M80 C90

M90 C50

M90 C50

49

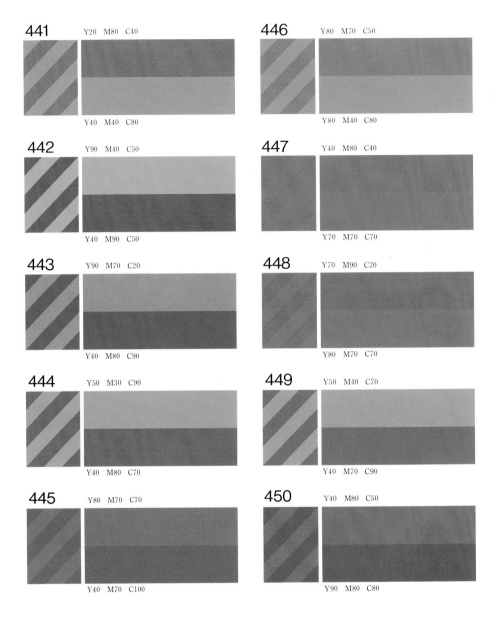

441 Y20 M80 C40 / Y40 M40 C80

446 Y80 M70 C50 / Y80 M40 C80

442 Y90 M40 C50 / Y40 M90 C50

447 Y40 M80 C40 / Y70 M70 C70

443 Y90 M70 C20 / Y40 M80 C90

448 Y70 M90 C20 / Y80 M70 C70

444 Y50 M30 C90 / Y40 M80 C70

449 Y50 M40 C70 / Y40 M70 C90

445 Y80 M70 C70 / Y40 M70 C100

450 Y40 M80 C50 / Y90 M80 C80

Medium Colors (continued)

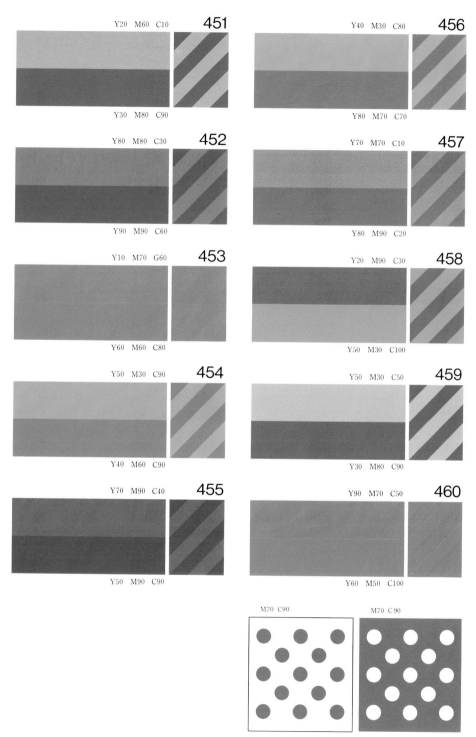

Y20 M60 C10 **451**

Y30 M80 C90

Y40 M30 C80 **456**

Y80 M70 C70

Y80 M80 C30 **452**

Y90 M90 C60

Y70 M70 C10 **457**

Y80 M90 C20

Y10 M70 G60 **453**

Y60 M60 C80

Y20 M90 C30 **458**

Y50 M30 C100

Y50 M30 C90 **454**

Y40 M60 C90

Y50 M30 C50 **459**

Y30 M80 C90

Y70 M90 C40 **455**

Y50 M90 C90

Y90 M70 C50 **460**

Y60 M50 C100

M70 C90

M70 C90

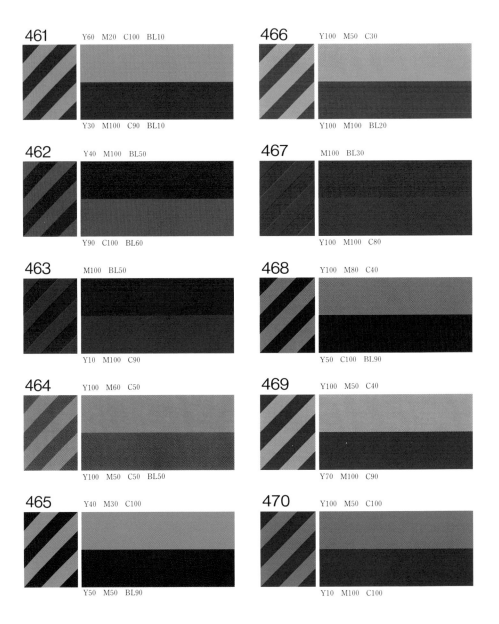

461   Y60 M20 C100 BL10

Y30 M100 C90 BL10

462   Y40 M100 BL50

Y90 C100 BL60

463   M100 BL50

Y10 M100 C90

464   Y100 M60 C50

Y100 M50 C50 BL50

465   Y40 M30 C100

Y50 M50 BL90

466   Y100 M50 C30

Y100 M100 BL20

467   M100 BL30

Y100 M100 C80

468   Y100 M80 C40

Y50 C100 BL90

469   Y100 M50 C40

Y70 M100 C90

470   Y100 M50 C100

Y10 M100 C100

Deep Colors

Colors in this category have a rich, luxurious quality which we seem to appreciate most in autumn. Analogies in material would be velvet or fine wool. They might be appropriate to suggest maturity, haute couture, country life, handmade sweaters, mystery, or romance.

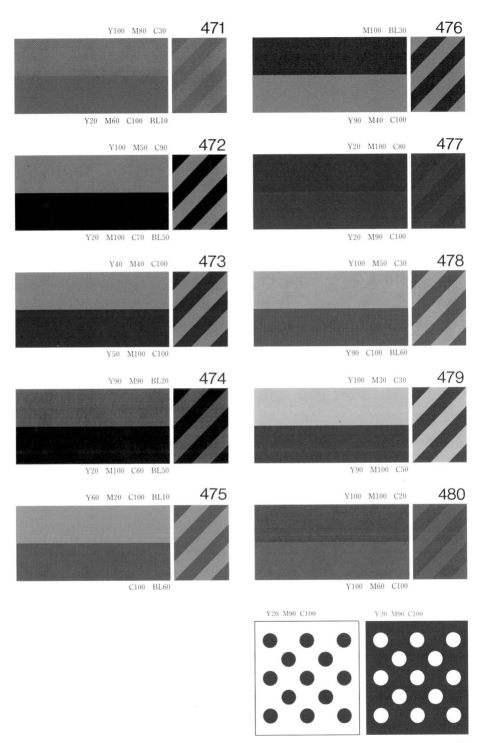

Y100 M80 C30 **471**

Y20 M60 C100 BL10

M100 BL30 **476**

Y90 M40 C100

Y100 M50 C90 **472**

Y20 M100 C70 BL50

Y20 M100 C80 **477**

Y20 M90 C100

Y40 M40 C100 **473**

Y50 M100 C100

Y100 M50 C30 **478**

Y90 C100 BL60

Y90 M90 BL20 **474**

Y20 M100 C60 BL50

Y100 M30 C30 **479**

Y90 M100 C50

Y60 M20 C100 BL10 **475**

C100 BL60

Y100 M100 C20 **480**

Y100 M60 C100

Y20 M90 C100

Y20 M90 C100

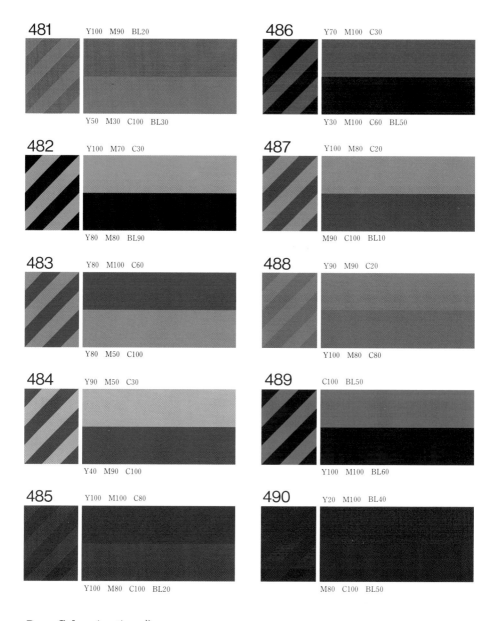

481 Y100 M90 BL20

Y50 M30 C100 BL30

486 Y70 M100 C30

Y30 M100 C60 BL50

482 Y100 M70 C30

Y80 M80 BL90

487 Y100 M80 C20

M90 C100 BL10

483 Y80 M100 C60

Y80 M50 C100

488 Y90 M90 C20

Y100 M80 C80

484 Y90 M50 C30

Y40 M90 C100

489 C100 BL50

Y100 M100 BL60

485 Y100 M100 C80

Y100 M80 C100 BL20

490 Y20 M100 BL40

M80 C100 BL50

Deep Colors (continued)

54

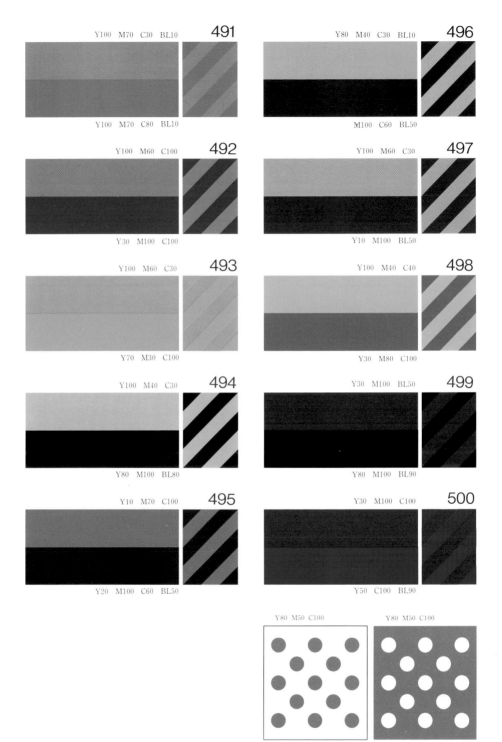

Y100 M70 C30 BL10 **491**

Y100 M70 C80 BL10

Y80 M40 C30 BL10 **496**

M100 C60 BL50

Y100 M60 C100 **492**

Y30 M100 C100

Y100 M60 C30 **497**

Y10 M100 BL50

Y100 M60 C30 **493**

Y70 M30 C100

Y100 M40 C40 **498**

Y30 M80 C100

Y100 M40 C30 **494**

Y80 M100 BL80

Y30 M100 BL50 **499**

Y80 M100 BL90

Y10 M70 C100 **495**

Y20 M100 C60 BL50

Y30 M100 C100 **500**

Y50 C100 BL90

Y80 M50 C100

Y80 M50 C100

55

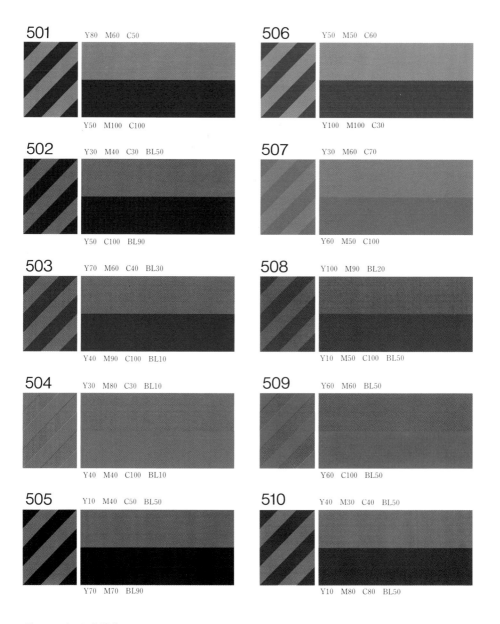

501 Y80 M60 C50
Y50 M100 C100

502 Y30 M40 C30 BL50
Y50 C100 BL90

503 Y70 M60 C40 BL30
Y40 M90 C100 BL10

504 Y30 M80 C30 BL10
Y40 M40 C100 BL10

505 Y10 M40 C50 BL50
Y70 M70 BL90

506 Y50 M50 C60
Y100 M100 C30

507 Y30 M60 C70
Y60 M50 C100

508 Y100 M90 BL20
Y10 M50 C100 BL50

509 Y60 M60 BL50
Y60 C100 BL50

510 Y40 M30 C40 BL50
Y10 M80 C80 BL50

Concentrated Colors
Both dark and a little dull, these colors are fall and winter fashion shades. They are rich, subdued, and elegant.

56

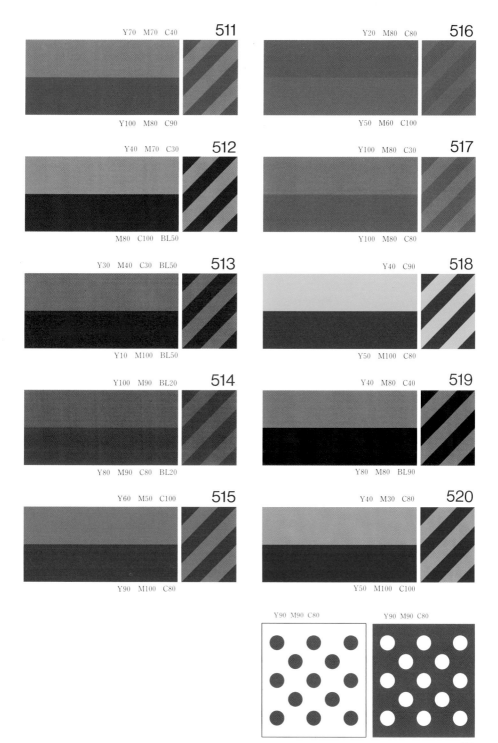

Y70 M70 C40 **511**
Y100 M80 C90

Y20 M80 C80 **516**
Y50 M60 C100

Y40 M70 C30 **512**
M80 C100 BL50

Y100 M80 C30 **517**
Y100 M80 C80

Y30 M40 C30 BL50 **513**
Y10 M100 BL50

Y40 C90 **518**
Y50 M100 C80

Y100 M90 BL20 **514**
Y80 M90 C80 BL20

Y40 M80 C40 **519**
Y80 M80 BL90

Y60 M50 C100 **515**
Y90 M100 C80

Y40 M30 C80 **520**
Y50 M100 C100

Y90 M90 C80

Y90 M90 C80

57

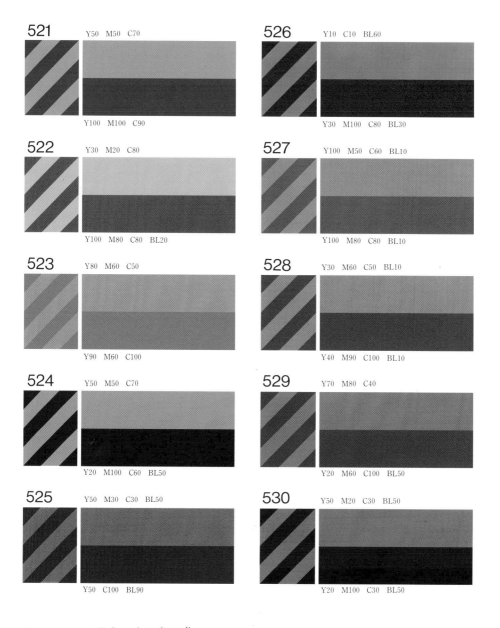

521 Y50 M50 C70

Y100 M100 C90

522 Y30 M20 C80

Y100 M80 C80 BL20

523 Y80 M60 C50

Y90 M60 C100

524 Y50 M50 C70

Y20 M100 C60 BL50

525 Y50 M30 C30 BL50

Y50 C100 BL90

526 Y10 C10 BL60

Y30 M100 C80 BL30

527 Y100 M50 C60 BL10

Y100 M80 C80 BL10

528 Y30 M60 C50 BL10

Y40 M90 C100 BL10

529 Y70 M80 C40

Y20 M60 C100 BL50

530 Y50 M20 C30 BL50

Y20 M100 C30 BL50

Concentrated Colors (continued)

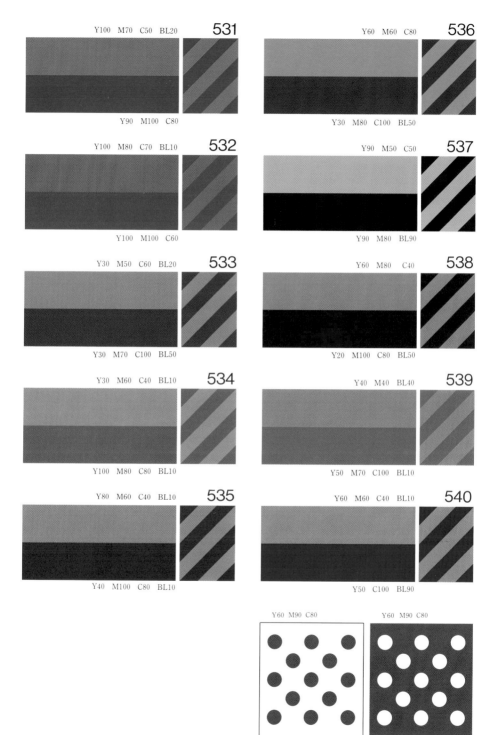

Y100 M70 C50 BL20 **531**

Y90 M100 C80

Y60 M60 C80 **536**

Y30 M80 C100 BL50

Y100 M80 C70 BL10 **532**

Y100 M100 C60

Y90 M50 C50 **537**

Y90 M80 BL90

Y30 M50 C60 BL20 **533**

Y30 M70 C100 BL50

Y60 M80 C40 **538**

Y20 M100 C80 BL50

Y30 M60 C40 BL10 **534**

Y100 M80 C80 BL10

Y40 M40 BL40 **539**

Y50 M70 C100 BL10

Y80 M60 C40 BL10 **535**

Y40 M100 C80 BL10

Y60 M60 C40 BL10 **540**

Y50 C100 BL90

Y60 M90 C80

Y60 M90 C80

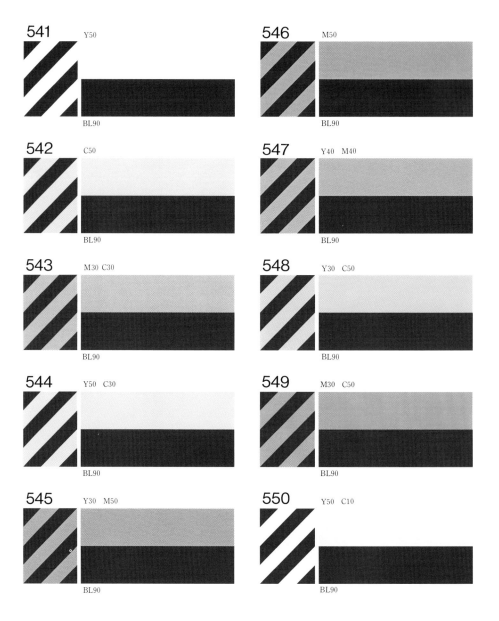

541 Y50 BL90

542 C50 BL90

543 M30 C30 BL90

544 Y50 C30 BL90

545 Y30 M50 BL90

546 M50 BL90

547 Y40 M40 BL90

548 Y30 C50 BL90

549 M30 C50 BL90

550 Y50 C10 BL90

Charcoal Gray

Called *sumi-iro* in Japanese, this gray is very close to black but creates a different tension. Its sensitive, sophisticated quality is well suited to formal wear. Contrasted here with bright colors, it can also create a soft and modern look. Use this gray when black would be too strong.

Y50 C10   **551**

Y70 M90 C80

Y10 C50   **556**

Y80 M80 BL90

Y40 C40   **552**

Y90 M80 C60 BL30

Y10 M50   **557**

Y70 M70 BL90

M50   **553**

Y90 M80 C100

Y60 C10   **558**

Y90 M100 C60

Y40 C60   **554**

Y100 M80 C80 BL10

Y50 C40   **559**

Y100 M60 C80 BL20

Y30 M30   **555**

Y100 M100 C80

M30 C30   **560**

Y80 M80 BL90

Bright with Concentrated Colors (1)

These color schemes demonstrate accentuated contrast.

Y50 M80 C100   Y50 M80 C100

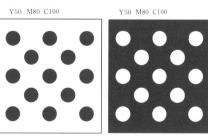

61

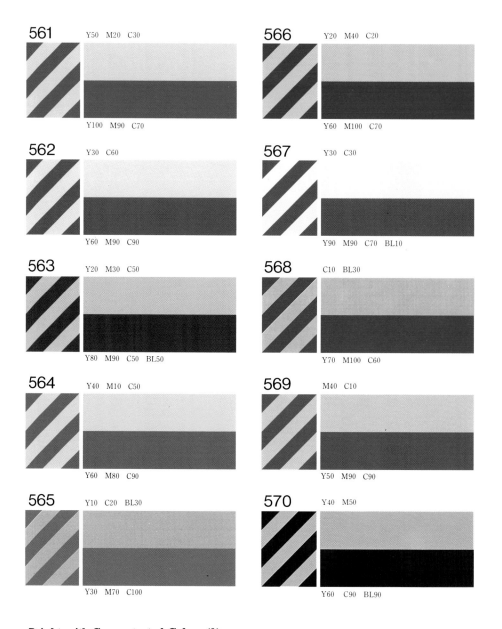

561 Y50 M20 C30

Y100 M90 C70

566 Y20 M40 C20

Y60 M100 C70

562 Y30 C60

Y60 M90 C90

567 Y30 C30

Y90 M90 C70 BL10

563 Y20 M30 C50

Y80 M90 C50 BL50

568 C10 BL30

Y70 M100 C60

564 Y40 M10 C50

Y60 M80 C90

569 M40 C10

Y50 M90 C90

565 Y10 C20 BL30

Y30 M70 C100

570 Y40 M50

Y60 C90 BL90

Bright with Concentrated Colors (1)
(continued)

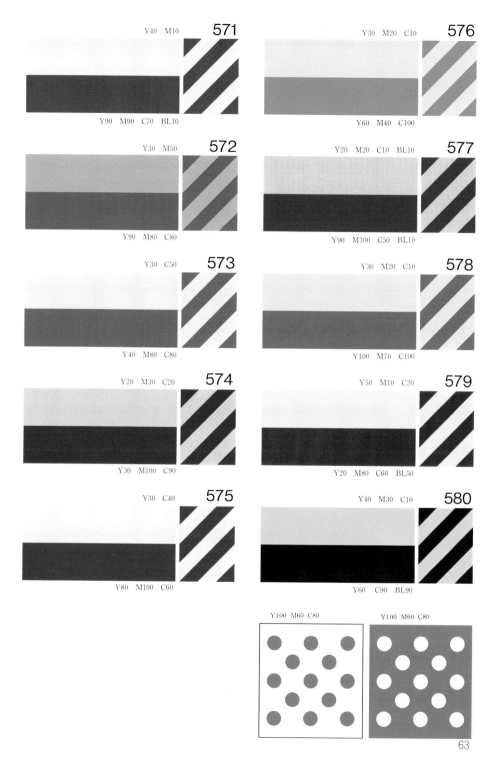

Y40 M10 **571**

Y90 M90 C70 BL10

Y30 M50 **572**

Y90 M80 C80

Y30 C50 **573**

Y40 M80 C80

Y20 M30 C20 **574**

Y30 M100 C90

Y30 C40 **575**

Y80 M100 C60

Y30 M20 C10 **576**

Y60 M40 C100

Y20 M20 C10 BL10 **577**

Y90 M100 C50 BL10

Y30 M20 C10 **578**

Y100 M70 C100

Y50 M10 C20 **579**

Y20 M80 C60 BL50

Y40 M30 C10 **580**

Y60 C90 BL90

Y100 M60 C80

Y100 M60 C80

63

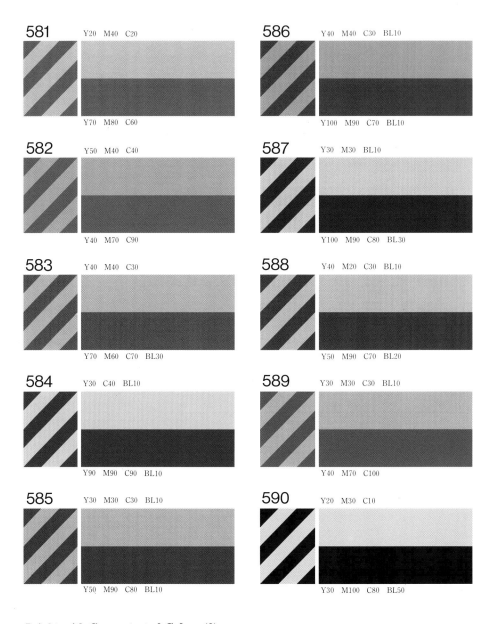

581 Y20 M40 C20

Y70 M80 C60

582 Y50 M40 C40

Y40 M70 C90

583 Y40 M40 C30

Y70 M60 C70 BL30

584 Y30 C40 BL10

Y90 M90 C90 BL10

585 Y30 M30 C30 BL10

Y50 M90 C80 BL10

586 Y40 M40 C30 BL10

Y100 M90 C70 BL10

587 Y30 M30 BL10

Y100 M90 C80 BL30

588 Y40 M20 C30 BL10

Y50 M90 C70 BL20

589 Y30 M30 C30 BL10

Y40 M70 C100

590 Y20 M30 C10

Y30 M100 C80 BL50

Bright with Concentrated Colors (2)
These color schemes contrast a dark
color with a subdued neutral color. On
page 64 are conservative shades and on
page 65, lighter colors. These colors
seem quiet, sedate, and elegant.

64

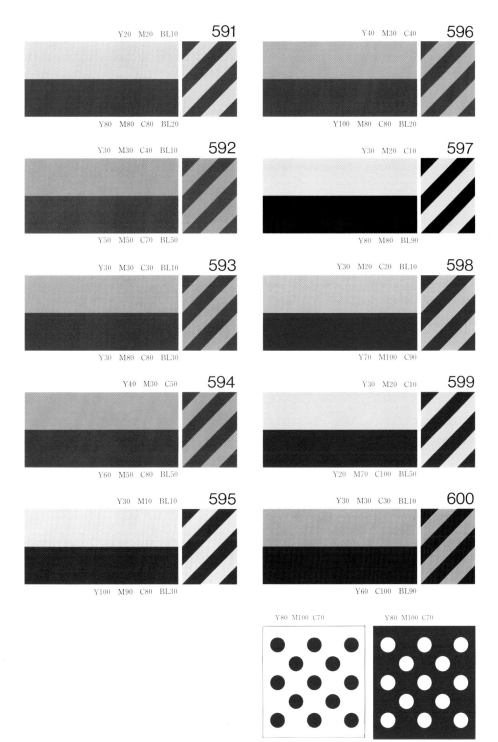

Y20 M20 BL10 **591**

Y80 M80 C80 BL20

Y40 M30 C40 **596**

Y100 M80 C80 BL20

Y30 M30 C40 BL10 **592**

Y50 M50 C70 BL50

Y30 M20 C10 **597**

Y80 M80 BL90

Y30 M30 C30 BL10 **593**

Y30 M80 C80 BL30

Y30 M20 C20 BL10 **598**

Y70 M100 C90

Y40 M30 C50 **594**

Y60 M50 C80 BL50

Y30 M20 C10 **599**

Y20 M70 C100 BL50

Y30 M10 BL10 **595**

Y100 M90 C80 BL30

Y30 M30 C30 BL10 **600**

Y60 C100 BL90

Y80 M100 C70

Y80 M100 C70

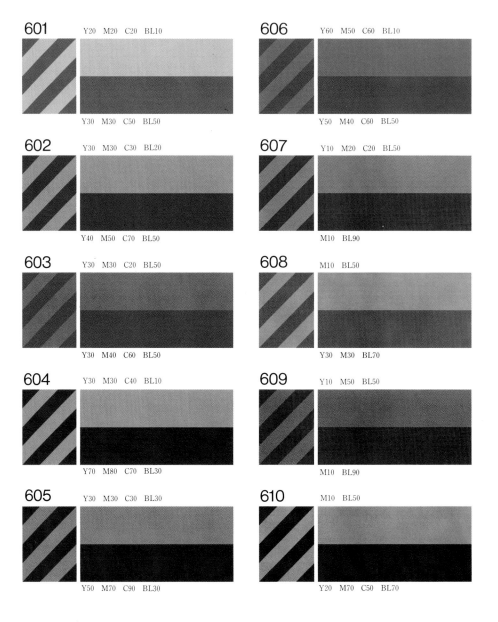

601   Y20   M20   C20   BL10
Y30   M30   C50   BL50

606   Y60   M50   C60   BL10
Y50   M40   C60   BL50

602   Y30   M30   C30   BL20
Y40   M50   C70   BL50

607   Y10   M20   C20   BL50
M10   BL90

603   Y30   M30   C20   BL50
Y30   M40   C60   BL50

608   M10   BL50
Y30   M30   BL70

604   Y30   M30   C40   BL10
Y70   M80   C70   BL30

609   Y10   M50   BL50
M10   BL90

605   Y30   M30   C30   BL30
Y50   M70   C90   BL30

610   M10   BL50
Y20   M70   C50   BL70

Subdued Colors

The colors on these pages have been greatly suppressed. Their grayish tones are not as easy to achieve as they appear. Two subdued but contrasting colors have been paired to bring out the colors even more strongly; for a more subdued effect, choose two related colors. While these are not youthful colors, their subtle dark contrasts could be used for summer fashions. These colors can be very satisfying. Pause a minute and consider the applications of such combinations as examples 628, 629, 633, or 640.

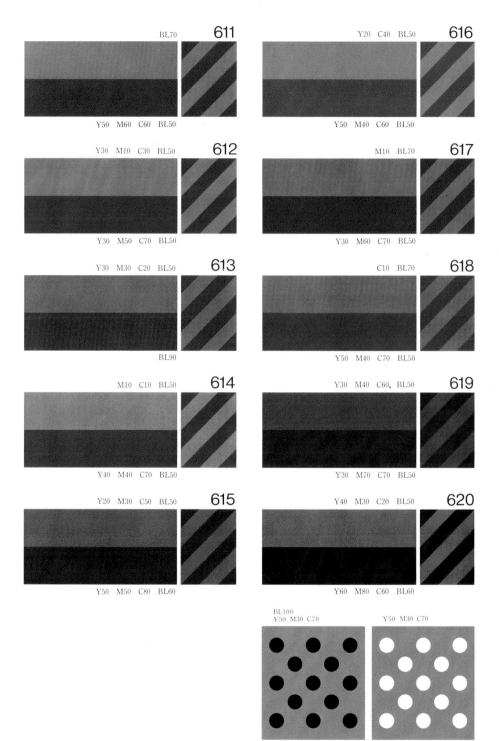

BL70   **611**

Y50 M60 C60 BL50

Y20 C40 BL50   **616**

Y50 M40 C60 BL50

Y30 M10 C30 BL50   **612**

Y30 M50 C70 BL50

M10 BL70   **617**

Y30 M60 C70 BL50

Y30 M30 C20 BL50   **613**

BL90

C10 BL70   **618**

Y50 M40 C70 BL50

M10 C10 BL50   **614**

Y40 M40 C70 BL50

Y30 M40 C60 BL50   **619**

Y30 M70 C70 BL50

Y20 M30 C50 BL50   **615**

Y50 M50 C80 BL60

Y40 M30 C20 BL50   **620**

Y60 M80 C60 BL60

BL100
Y50 M30 C70

Y50 M30 C70

67

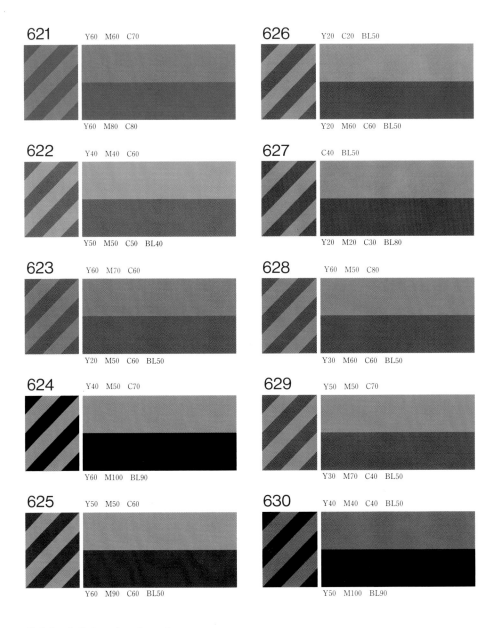

621   Y60   M60   C70

Y60   M80   C80

622   Y40   M40   C60

Y50   M50   C50   BL40

623   Y60   M70   C60

Y20   M50   C60   BL50

624   Y40   M50   C70

Y60   M100   BL90

625   Y50   M50   C60

Y60   M90   C60   BL50

626   Y20   C20   BL50

Y20   M60   C60   BL50

627   C40   BL50

Y20   M20   C30   BL80

628   Y60   M50   C80

Y30   M60   C60   BL50

629   Y50   M50   C70

Y30   M70   C40   BL50

630   Y40   M40   C40   BL50

Y50   M100   BL90

Subdued Colors (continued)

68

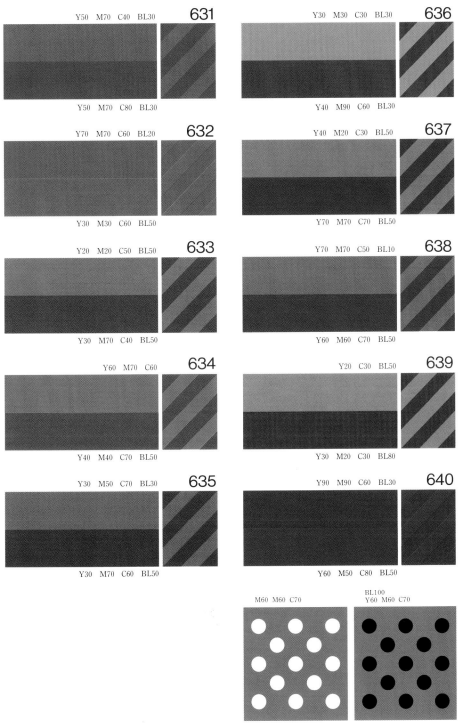

Y50 M70 C40 BL30 **631**

Y50 M70 C80 BL30

Y30 M30 C30 BL30 **636**

Y40 M90 C60 BL30

Y70 M70 C60 BL20 **632**

Y30 M30 C60 BL50

Y40 M20 C30 BL50 **637**

Y70 M70 C70 BL50

Y20 M20 C50 BL50 **633**

Y30 M70 C40 BL50

Y70 M70 C50 BL10 **638**

Y60 M60 C70 BL50

Y60 M70 C60 **634**

Y40 M40 C70 BL50

Y20 C30 BL50 **639**

Y30 M20 C30 BL80

Y30 M50 C70 BL30 **635**

Y30 M70 C60 BL50

Y90 M90 C60 BL30 **640**

Y60 M50 C80 BL50

M60 M60 C70

BL100
Y60 M60 C70

69

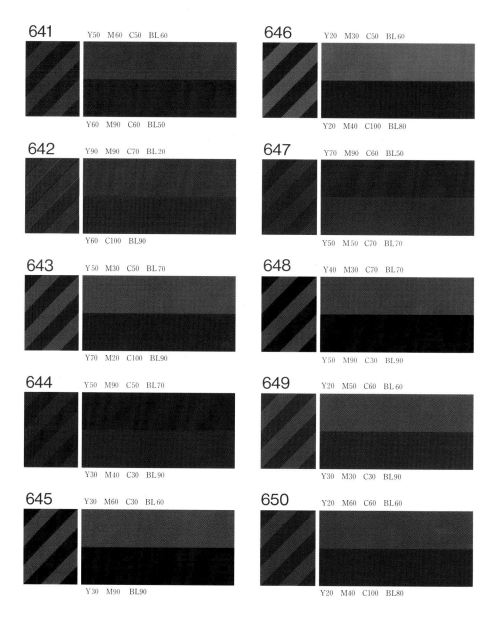

641 Y50 M60 C50 BL60
Y60 M90 C60 BL50

642 Y90 M90 C70 BL20
Y60 C100 BL90

643 Y50 M30 C50 BL70
Y70 M20 C100 BL90

644 Y50 M90 C50 BL70
Y30 M40 C30 BL90

645 Y30 M60 C30 BL60
Y30 M90 BL90

646 Y20 M30 C50 BL60
Y20 M40 C100 BL80

647 Y70 M90 C60 BL50
Y50 M50 C70 BL70

648 Y40 M30 C70 BL70
Y50 M90 C30 BL90

649 Y20 M50 C60 BL60
Y30 M30 C30 BL90

650 Y20 M60 C60 BL60
Y20 M40 C100 BL80

Dark Colors

The combination of two dark colors creates a beautiful, rich fall/winter color scheme. The colors are orderly, serious, refined, and extremely handsome.

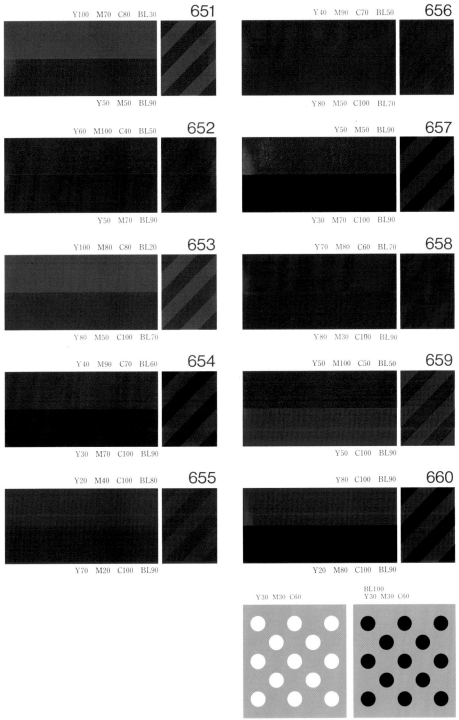

651 Y100 M70 C80 BL30

Y50 M50 BL90

656 Y40 M90 C70 BL50

Y80 M50 C100 BL70

652 Y60 M100 C40 BL50

Y50 M70 BL90

657 Y50 M50 BL90

Y30 M70 C100 BL90

653 Y100 M80 C80 BL20

Y80 M50 C100 BL70

658 Y70 M80 C60 BL70

Y80 M30 C100 BL90

654 Y40 M90 C70 BL60

Y30 M70 C100 BL90

659 Y50 M100 C50 BL50

Y50 C100 BL90

655 Y20 M40 C100 BL80

Y70 M20 C100 BL90

660 Y80 C100 BL90

Y20 M80 C100 BL90

Y30 M30 C60

BL100
Y30 M30 C60

71

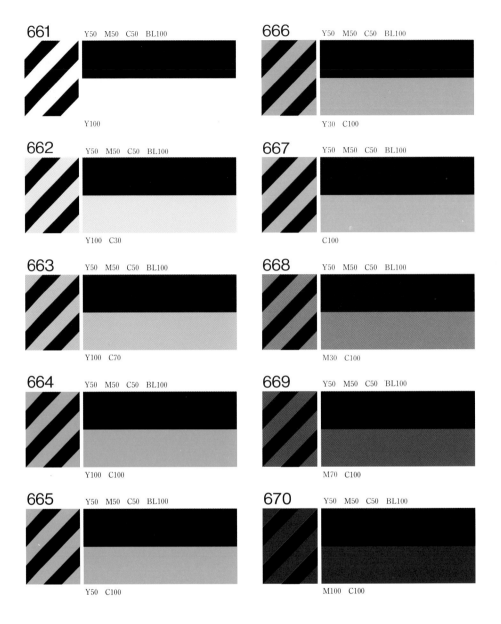

661   Y50   M50   C50   BL100

Y100

662   Y50   M50   C50   BL100

Y100   C30

663   Y50   M50   C50   BL100

Y100   C70

664   Y50   M50   C50   BL100

Y100   C100

665   Y50   M50   C50   BL100

Y50   C100

666   Y50   M50   C50   BL100

Y30   C100

667   Y50   M50   C50   BL100

C100

668   Y50   M50   C50   BL100

M30   C100

669   Y50   M50   C50   BL100

M70   C100

670   Y50   M50   C50   BL100

M100   C100

Black with Vivid Colors

Black has chameleon characteristics, depending on the material used; its tones will vary from reddish black to bluish black and look entirely different on velvet and cotton. In fashion it's essential to consider the fabric, the color tone, and the design when using black. "School bus yellow" and black, as in example 680, is con- sidered to be the most visible color combination that we use.

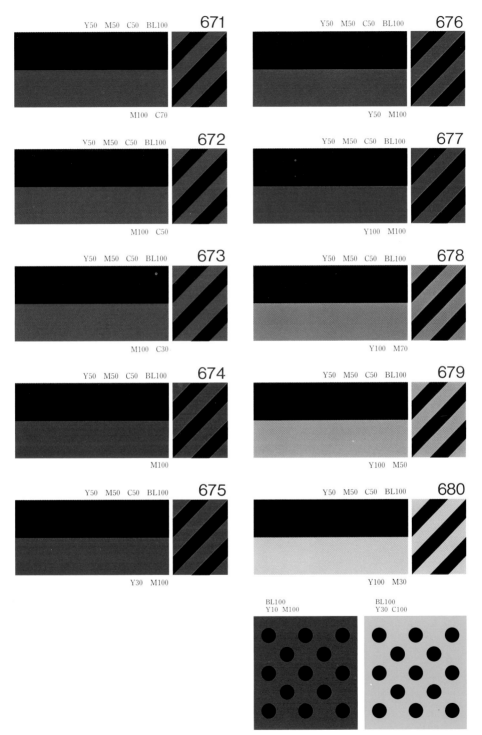

Y50 M50 C50 BL100 **671**

M100 C70

Y50 M50 C50 BL100 **676**

Y50 M100

V50 M50 C50 BL100 **672**

M100 C50

Y50 M50 C50 BL100 **677**

Y100 M100

Y50 M50 C50 BL100 **673**

M100 C30

Y50 M50 C50 BL100 **678**

Y100 M70

Y50 M50 C50 BL100 **674**

M100

Y50 M50 C50 BL100 **679**

Y100 M50

Y50 M50 C50 BL100 **675**

Y30 M100

Y50 M50 C50 BL100 **680**

Y100 M30

BL100
Y10 M100

BL100
Y30 C100

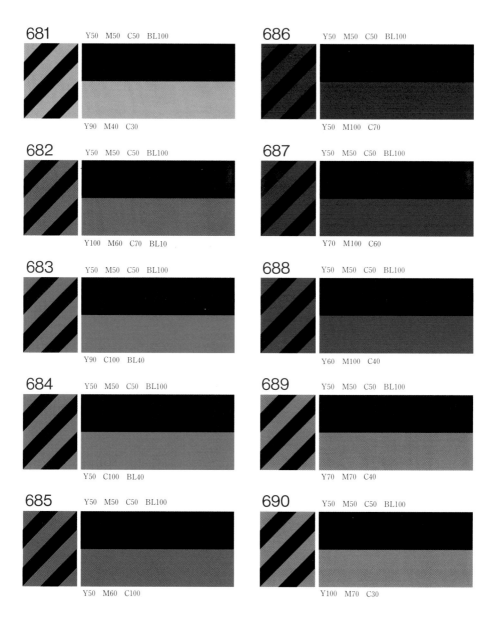

| 681 | Y50 M50 C50 BL100 | 686 | Y50 M50 C50 BL100 |
| Y90 M40 C30 | | Y50 M100 C70 | |

681 Y50 M50 C50 BL100 / Y90 M40 C30

682 Y50 M50 C50 BL100 / Y100 M60 C70 BL10

683 Y50 M50 C50 BL100 / Y90 C100 BL40

684 Y50 M50 C50 BL100 / Y50 C100 BL40

685 Y50 M50 C50 BL100 / Y50 M60 C100

686 Y50 M50 C50 BL100 / Y50 M100 C70

687 Y50 M50 C50 BL100 / Y70 M100 C60

688 Y50 M50 C50 BL100 / Y60 M100 C40

689 Y50 M50 C50 BL100 / Y70 M70 C40

690 Y50 M50 C50 BL100 / Y100 M70 C30

Black with Concentrated Colors

By darkening the color paired with black, the color scheme gains stability. Black is a basic fashion color that imparts calmness and richness to any color scheme. Calmness, mystery, and maturity are suggested and reinforced by the use of black with certain colors.

74

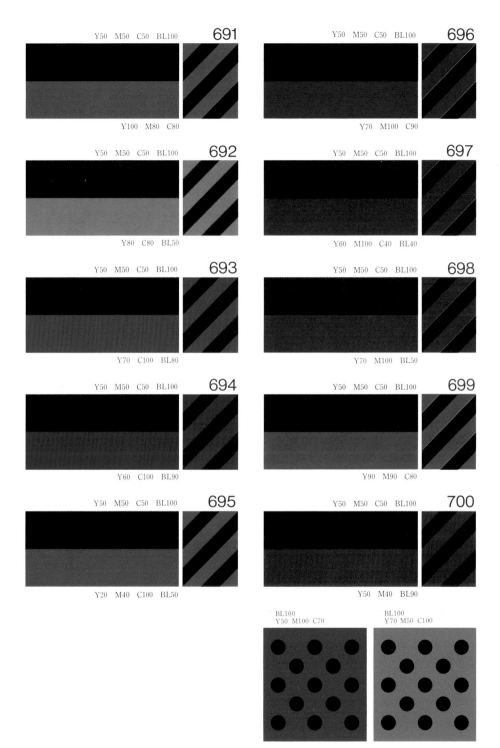

Y50 M50 C50 BL100 **691**

Y100 M80 C80

Y50 M50 C50 BL100 **692**

Y80 C80 BL50

Y50 M50 C50 BL100 **693**

Y70 C100 BL80

Y50 M50 C50 BL100 **694**

Y60 C100 BL90

Y50 M50 C50 BL100 **695**

Y20 M40 C100 BL50

Y50 M50 C50 BL100 **696**

Y70 M100 C90

Y50 M50 C50 BL100 **697**

Y60 M100 C40 BL40

Y50 M50 C50 BL100 **698**

Y70 M100 BL50

Y50 M50 C50 BL100 **699**

Y90 M90 C80

Y50 M50 C50 BL100 **700**

Y50 M40 BL90

BL100
Y50 M100 C70

BL100
Y70 M50 C100

75

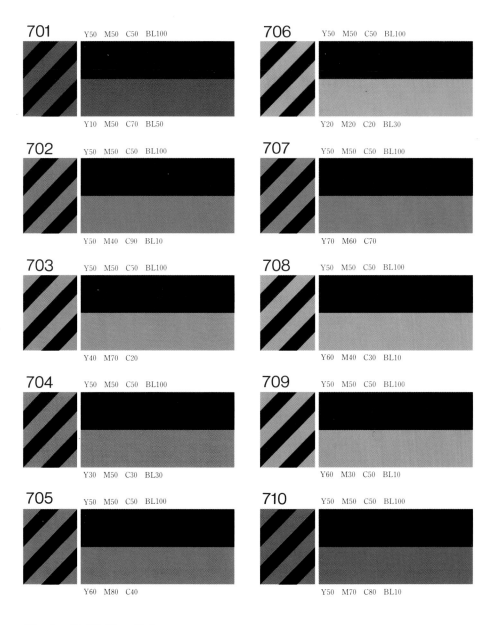

701 Y50 M50 C50 BL100

Y10 M50 C70 BL50

702 Y50 M50 C50 BL100

Y50 M40 C90 BL10

703 Y50 M50 C50 BL100

Y40 M70 C20

704 Y50 M50 C50 BL100

Y30 M50 C30 BL30

705 Y50 M50 C50 BL100

Y60 M80 C40

706 Y50 M50 C50 BL100

Y20 M20 C20 BL30

707 Y50 M50 C50 BL100

Y70 M60 C70

708 Y50 M50 C50 BL100

Y60 M40 C30 BL10

709 Y50 M50 C50 BL100

Y60 M30 C50 BL10

710 Y50 M50 C50 BL100

Y50 M70 C80 BL10

Black with Medium Colors

Black always intensifies the color it is paired with: in combination with a dull sober tone, it makes an agreeable, formal, stable color scheme. With some of these colors, black suggests art deco color motifs.

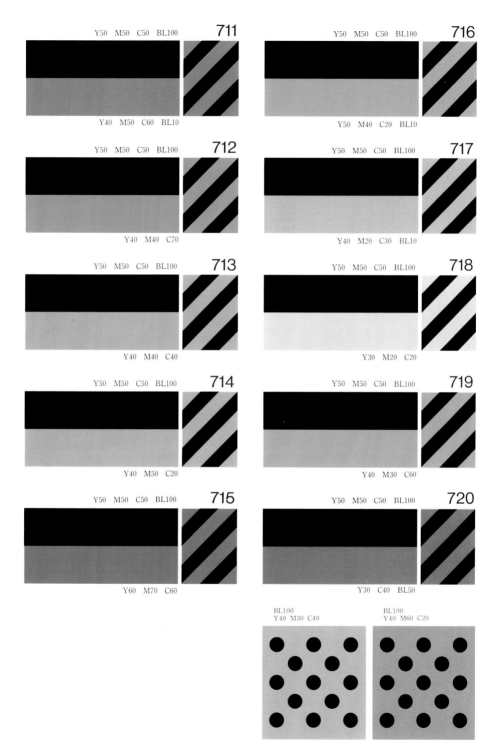

Y50 M50 C50 BL100 **711**

Y40 M50 C60 BL10

Y50 M50 C50 BL100 **716**

Y50 M40 C20 BL10

Y50 M50 C50 BL100 **712**

Y40 M40 C70

Y50 M50 C50 BL100 **717**

Y40 M20 C30 BL10

Y50 M50 C50 BL100 **713**

Y40 M40 C40

Y50 M50 C50 BL100 **718**

Y30 M20 C20

Y50 M50 C50 BL100 **714**

Y40 M50 C20

Y50 M50 C50 BL100 **719**

Y40 M30 C60

Y50 M50 C50 BL100 **715**

Y60 M70 C60

Y50 M50 C50 BL100 **720**

Y30 C40 BL50

BL100
Y40 M30 C40

BL100
Y40 M60 C20

77

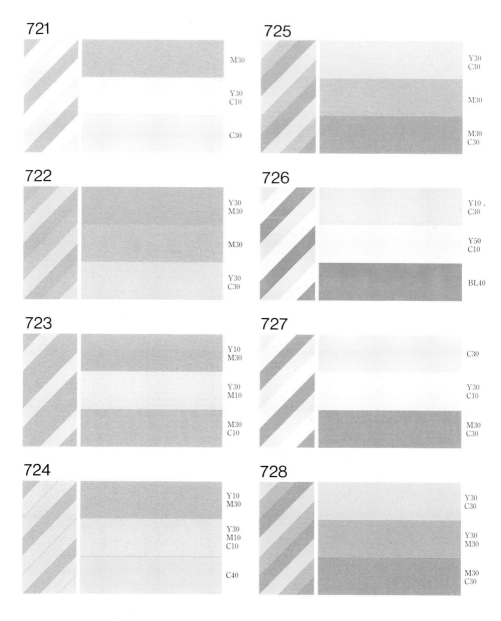

721
M30
Y30 C10
C30

725
Y30 C30
M30
M30 C30

722
Y30 M30
M30
Y30 C30

726
Y10 . C30
Y50 C10
BL40

723
Y10 M30
Y30 M10
M30 C10

727
C30
Y30 C10
M30 C30

724
Y10 M30
Y30 M10 C10
C40

728
Y30 C30
Y30 M30
M30 C30

Pale Colors
It is important when working with these colors to strive for a feeling of unity. It is best to control the general tone and, in the case of similar colors, to choose ones with varying degrees of brightness.

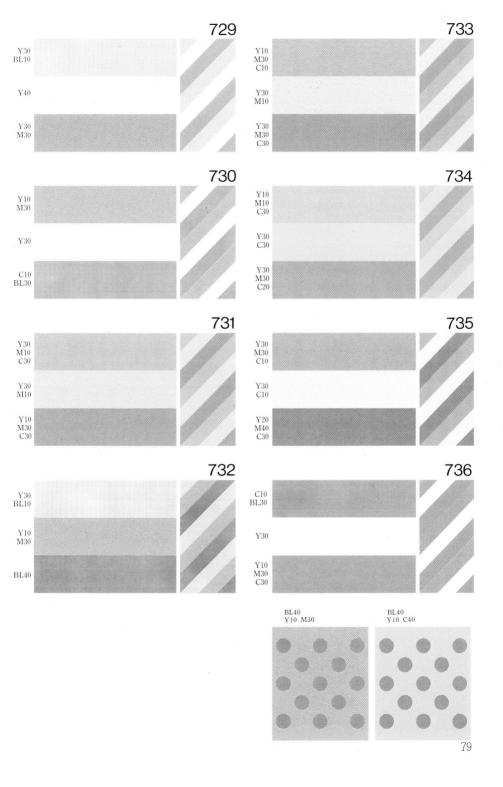

729

Y30
BL10

Y40

Y30
M30

730

Y10
M30

Y30

C10
BL30

731

Y30
M10
C30

Y30
M10

Y10
M30
C30

732

Y30
BL10

Y10
M30

BL40

733

Y10
M30
C10

Y30
M10

Y30
M30
C30

734

Y10
M10
C30

Y30
C30

Y30
M30
C20

735

Y30
M30
C10

Y30
C10

Y20
M40
C30

736

C10
BL30

Y30

Y10
M30
C30

BL40
Y10 M30

BL40
Y10 C40

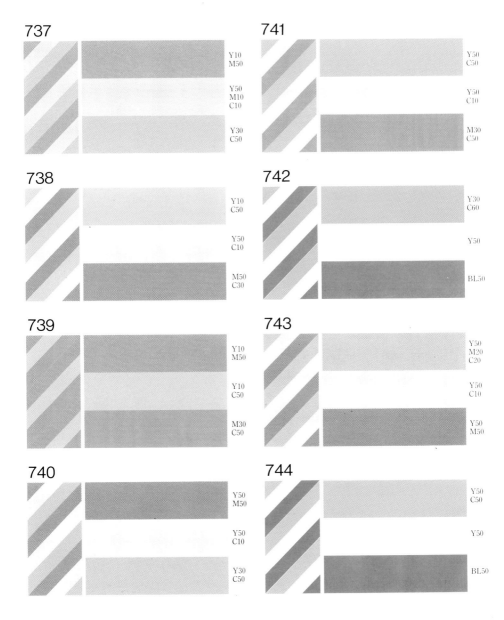

737

	Y10 M50
	Y50 M10 C10
	Y30 C50

741

	Y50 C50
	Y50 C10
	M30 C50

738

	Y10 C50
	Y50 C10
	M50 C30

742

	Y30 C60
	Y50
	BL50

739

	Y10 M50
	Y10 C50
	M30 C50

743

	Y50 M20 C20
	Y50 C10
	Y50 M50

740

	Y50 M50
	Y50 C10
	Y30 C50

744

	Y50 C50
	Y50
	BL50

Bright Colors

These sweet spring colors have the light-heartedness of an amusement park. Consider here not only the color combination but also the balance of brightness and brilliance of the overall color scheme.

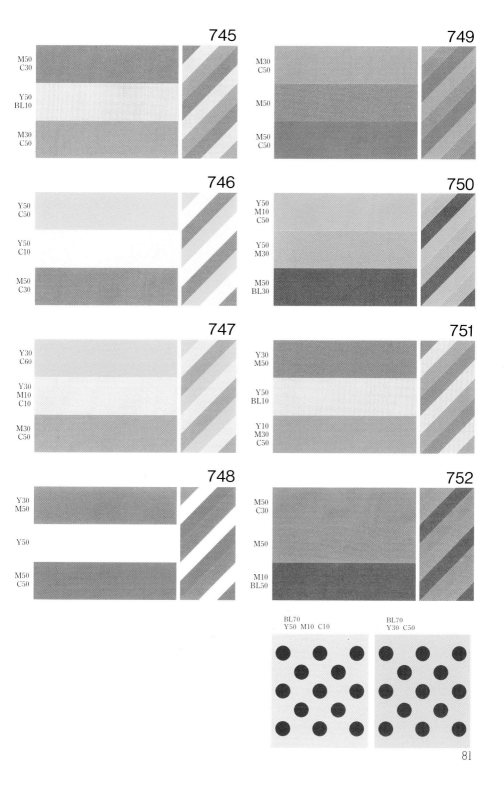

745

M50
C30

Y50
BL10

M30
C50

746

Y50
C50

Y50
C10

M50
C30

747

Y30
C60

Y30
M10
C10

M30
C50

748

Y30
M50

Y50

M50
C50

749

M30
C50

M50

M50
C50

750

Y50
M10
C50

Y50
M30

M50
BL30

751

Y30
M50

Y50
BL10

Y10
M30
C50

752

M50
C30

M50

M10
BL50

BL70
Y50 M10 C10

BL70
Y30 C50

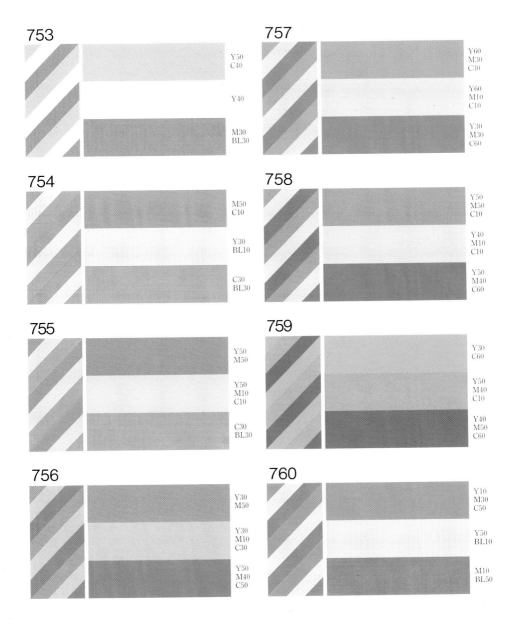

753

Y50
C40

Y40

M30
BL30

757

Y60
M30
C30

Y60
M10
C10

Y30
M30
C60

754

M50
C10

Y30
BL10

C30
BL30

758

Y50
M50
C10

Y40
M10
C10

Y50
M40
C60

755

Y50
M50

Y50
M10
C10

C30
BL30

759

Y30
C60

Y50
M40
C10

Y40
M50
C60

756

Y30
M50

Y30
M10
C30

Y50
M40
C50

760

Y10
M30
C50

Y50
BL10

M10
BL50

Bright Colors (continued)

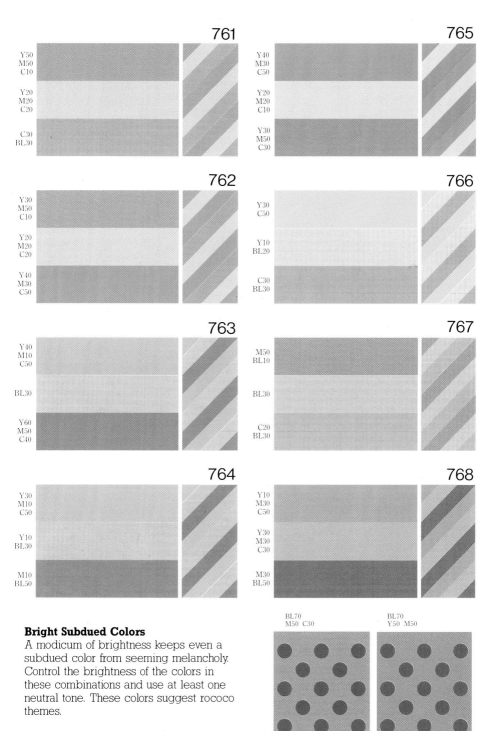

761

Y50
M50
C10

Y20
M20
C20

C30
BL30

765

Y40
M30
C50

Y20
M20
C10

Y30
M50
C30

762

Y30
M50
C10

Y20
M20
C20

Y40
M30
C50

766

Y30
C50

Y10
BL20

C30
BL30

763

Y40
M10
C50

BL30

Y60
M50
C40

767

M50
BL10

BL30

C20
BL30

764

Y30
M10
C50

Y10
BL30

M10
BL50

768

Y10
M30
C50

Y30
M30
C30

M30
BL50

Bright Subdued Colors

A modicum of brightness keeps even a subdued color from seeming melancholy. Control the brightness of the colors in these combinations and use at least one neutral tone. These colors suggest rococo themes.

BL70
M50 C30

BL70
Y50 M50

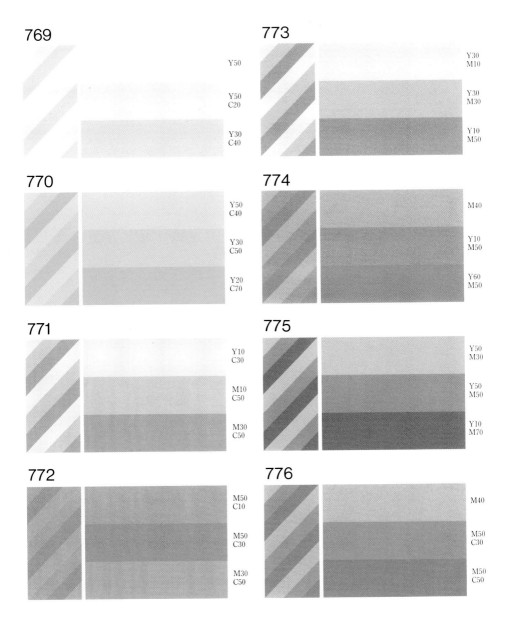

769

Y50

Y50
C20

Y30
C40

770

Y50
C40

Y30
C50

Y20
C70

771

Y10
C30

M10
C50

M30
C50

772

M50
C10

M50
C30

M30
C50

773

Y30
M10

Y30
M30

Y10
M50

774

M40

Y10
M50

Y60
M50

775

Y50
M30

Y50
M50

Y10
M70

776

M40

M50
C30

M50
C50

Effects of Gradation

Combining gradations of the same color is a breeze: as long as the tones have an overall harmony and vary enough to avoid a monotone look, the color scheme will have colorful, deep tones. Springlike sherbet tones stand out well with this technique.

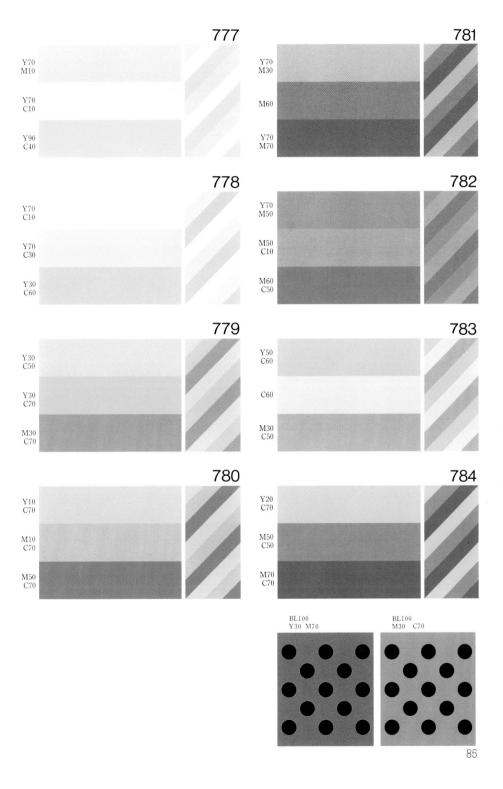

777

Y70
M10

Y70
C10

Y90
C40

778

Y70
C10

Y70
C30

Y30
C60

779

Y30
C50

Y30
C70

M30
C70

780

Y10
C70

M10
C70

M50
C70

781

Y70
M30

M60

Y70
M70

782

Y70
M50

M50
C10

M60
C50

783

Y50
C60

C60

M30
C50

784

Y20
C70

M50
C50

M70
C70

BL100
Y30 M70

BL100
M30 C70

85

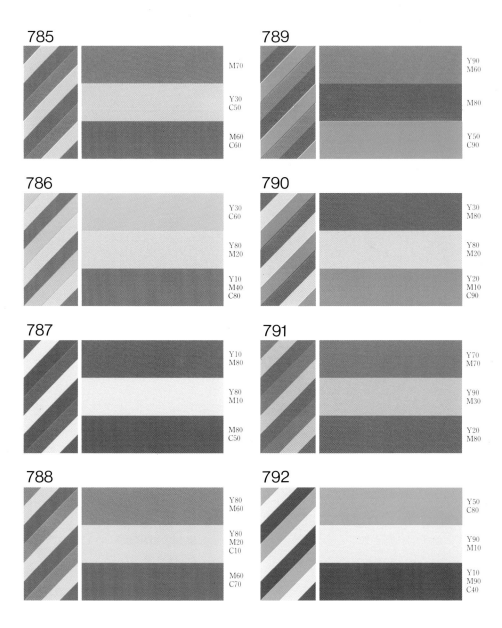

785

M70

Y30
C50

M60
C60

786

Y30
C60

Y80
M20

Y10
M40
C80

787

Y10
M80

Y80
M10

M80
C50

788

Y80
M60

Y80
M20
C10

M60
C70

789

Y90
M60

M80

Y50
C90

790

Y30
M80

Y80
M20

Y20
M10
C90

791

Y70
M70

Y90
M30

Y20
M80

792

Y50
C80

Y90
M10

Y10
M90
C40

Bright Vivid Colors
Full of brilliance and light, the colors in
this group are often matched with white
for a healthy summer look. These colors
suggest energy, sporting activities, and
toys.

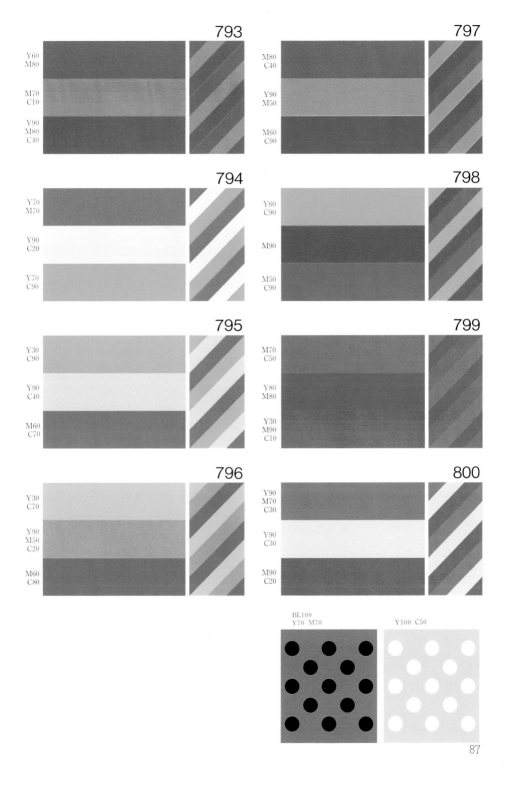

793

Y60 M80

M70 C10

Y90 M80 C40

794

Y70 M70

Y90 C20

Y70 C90

795

Y30 C90

Y90 C40

M60 C70

796

Y30 C70

Y90 M50 C20

M60 C80

797

M80 C40

Y90 M50

M60 C90

798

Y60 C90

M90

M50 C90

799

M70 C50

Y80 M80

Y30 M90 C10

800

Y90 M70 C30

Y90 C30

M90 C20

BL100
Y70 M70

Y100 C50

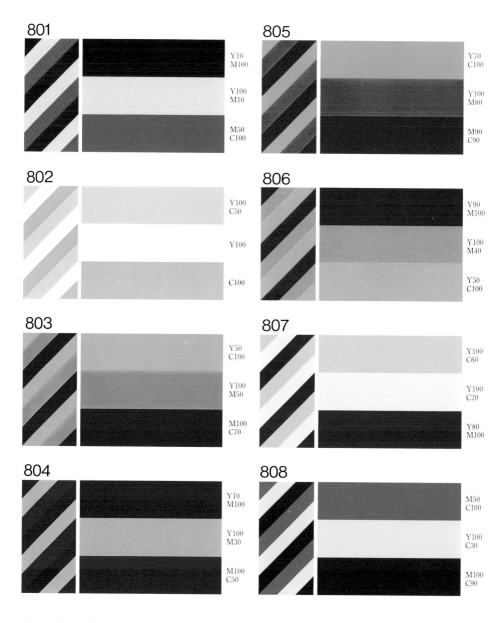

801

Y10
M100

Y100
M10

M50
C100

805

Y70
C100

Y100
M80

M90
C90

802

Y100
C50

Y100

C100

806

Y90
M100

Y100
M40

Y50
C100

803

Y50
C100

Y100
M50

M100
C70

807

Y100
C60

Y100
C20

Y80
M100

804

Y10
M100

Y100
M30

M100
C50

808

M50
C100

Y100
C30

M100
C90

More Vivid Colors
Bold use of these color schemes has a
very strong effect, because each of the
colors has very distinct and brilliant
characteristics.

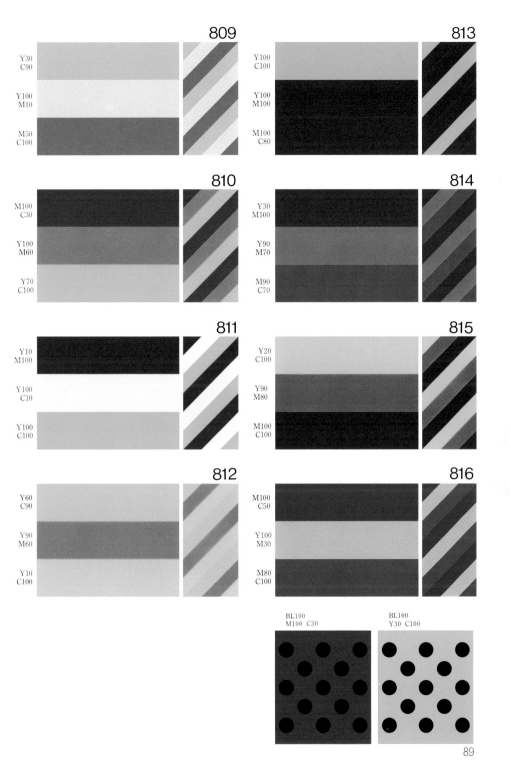

809

Y30
C90

Y100
M10

M50
C100

813

Y100
C100

Y100
M100

M100
C80

810

M100
C30

Y100
M60

Y70
C100

814

Y30
M100

Y90
M70

M90
C70

811

Y10
M100

Y100
C10

Y100
C100

815

Y20
C100

Y90
M80

M100
C100

812

Y60
C90

Y90
M60

Y10
C100

816

M100
C50

Y100
M30

M80
C100

BL100
M100 C30

BL100
Y30 C100

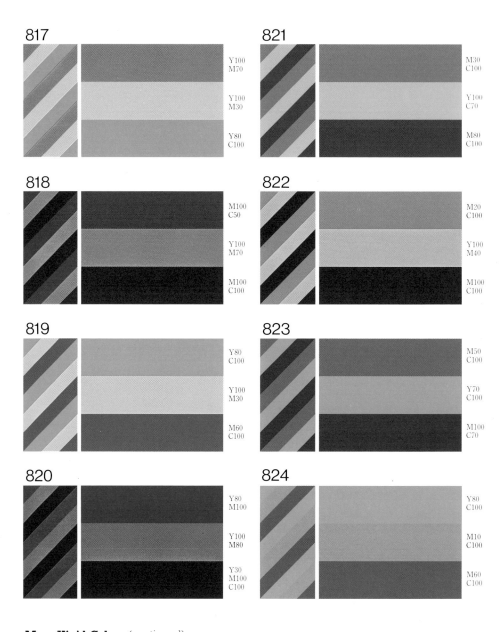

817

Y100
M70

Y100
M30

Y80
C100

821

M30
C100

Y100
C70

M80
C100

818

M100
C50

Y100
M70

M100
C100

822

M20
C100

Y100
M40

M100
C100

819

Y80
C100

Y100
M30

M60
C100

823

M50
C100

Y70
C100

M100
C70

820

Y80
M100

Y100
M80

Y30
M100
C100

824

Y80
C100

M10
C100

M60
C100

More Vivid Colors (continued)

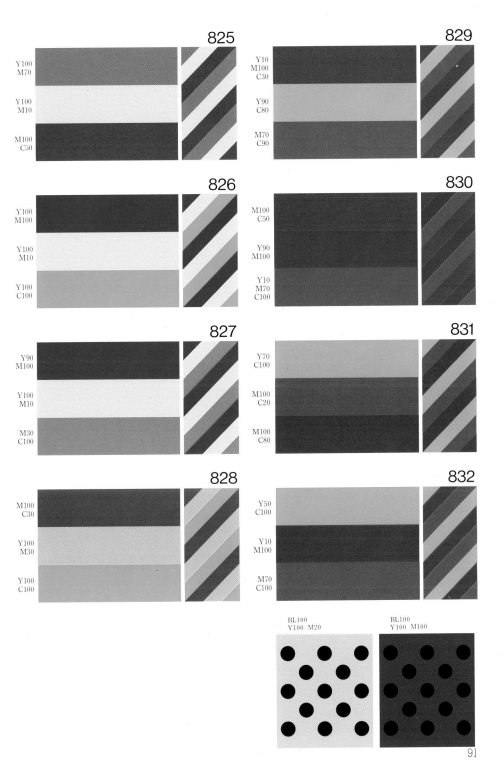

825
Y100 M70
Y100 M10
M100 C50

829
Y10 M100 C30
Y90 C80
M70 C90

826
Y100 M100
Y100 M10
Y100 C100

830
M100 C50
Y90 M100
Y10 M70 C100

827
Y90 M100
Y100 M10
M30 C100

831
Y70 C100
M100 C20
M100 C80

828
M100 C30
Y100 M30
Y100 C100

832
Y50 C100
Y10 M100
M70 C100

BL100 Y100 M20

BL100 Y100 M100

91

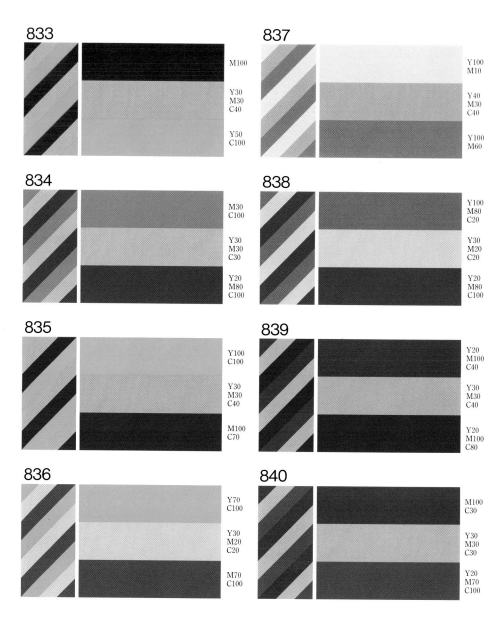

833

M100

Y30
M30
C40

Y50
C100

837

Y100
M10

Y40
M30
C40

Y100
M60

834

M30
C100

Y30
M30
C30

Y20
M80
C100

838

Y100
M80
C20

Y30
M20
C20

Y20
M80
C100

835

Y100
C100

Y30
M30
C40

M100
C70

839

Y20
M100
C40

Y30
M30
C40

Y20
M100
C80

836

Y70
C100

Y30
M20
C20

M70
C100

840

M100
C30

Y30
M30
C30

Y20
M70
C100

Vivid Colors plus a Neutral
One color scheme technique is to separate bright colors: colors are softened by adding a gray, emphasized by adding black. Here a beige (which has the same effect as gray) has been placed between two strong primary colors. The overall effect is muted and quite elegant.

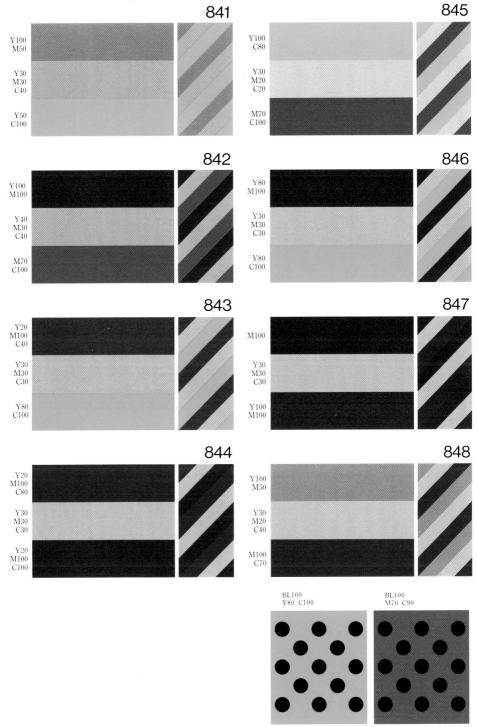

841

Y100
M50

Y30
M30
C40

Y50
C100

842

Y100
M100

Y40
M30
C40

M70
C100

843

Y20
M100
C40

Y30
M30
C30

Y80
C100

844

Y20
M100
C80

Y30
M30
C30

Y20
M100
C100

845

Y100
C80

Y30
M20
C20

M70
C100

846

Y80
M100

Y30
M30
C30

Y80
C100

847

M100

Y30
M30
C30

Y100
M100

848

Y100
M50

Y30
M20
C40

M100
C70

BL100
Y80 C100

BL100
M70 C90

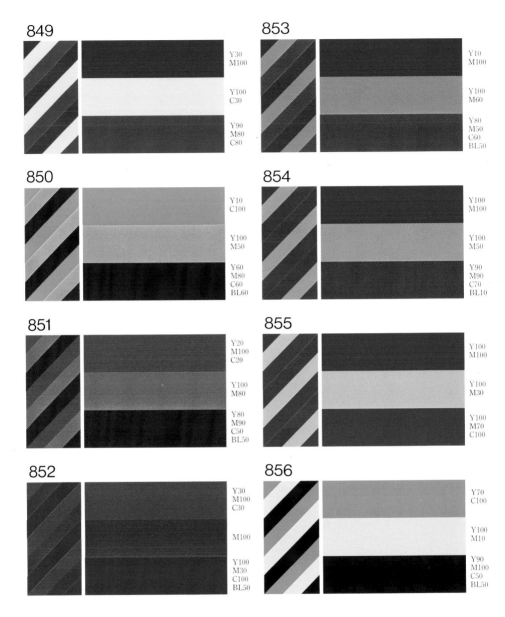

849

Y30
M100

Y100
C30

Y90
M80
C80

853

Y10
M100

Y100
M60

Y80
M50
C60
BL50

850

Y10
C100

Y100
M50

Y60
M80
C60
BL60

854

Y100
M100

Y100
M50

Y90
M90
C70
BL10

851

Y20
M100
C20

Y100
M80

Y80
M90
C50
BL50

855

Y100
M100

Y100
M30

Y100
M70
C100

852

Y30
M100
C30

M100

Y100
M30
C100
BL50

856

Y70
C100

Y100
M10

Y90
M100
C50
BL50

Vivid Color plus
Concentrated Color (1)

The dark color at the bottom serves to tie
the three colors together. Browns, like
black and gray, are easy to use with
other colors. Among this group are many
hot, African colors in pleasing color
combinations.

94

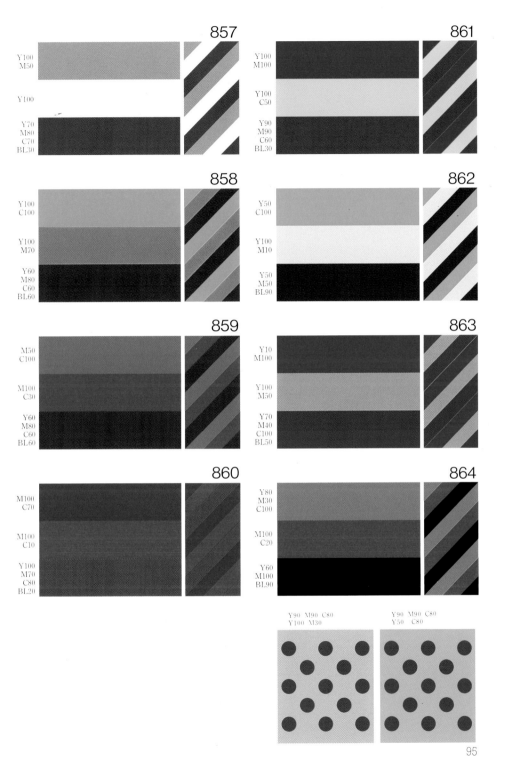

857

Y100
M50

Y100

Y70
M80
C70
BL30

861

Y100
M100

Y100
C50

Y90
M90
C60
BL30

858

Y100
C100

Y100
M70

Y60
M80
C60
BL60

862

Y50
C100

Y100
M10

Y50
M50
BL90

859

M50
C100

M100
C30

Y60
M80
C60
BL60

863

Y10
M100

Y100
M50

Y70
M40
C100
BL50

860

M100
C70

M100
C10

Y100
M70
C80
BL20

864

Y80
M30
C100

M100
C20

Y60
M100
BL90

Y90 M90 C80
Y100 M30

Y90 M90 C80
Y50 C80

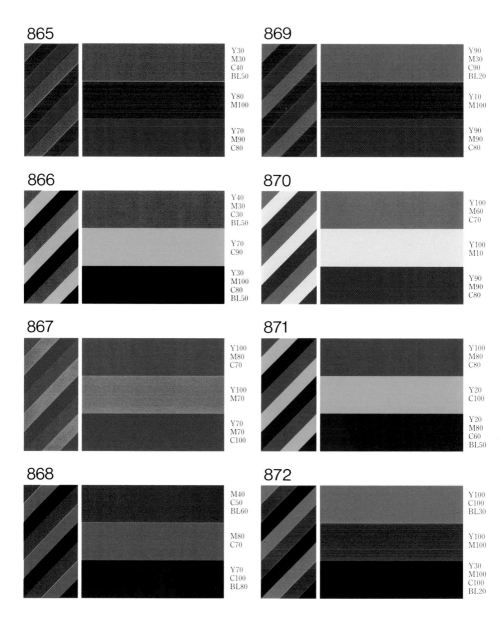

865

Y30
M30
C40
BL50

Y80
M100

Y70
M90
C80

869

Y90
M30
C90
BL20

Y10
M100

Y90
M90
C80

866

Y40
M30
C30
BL50

Y70
C90

Y30
M100
C80
BL50

870

Y100
M60
C70

Y100
M10

Y90
M90
C80

867

Y100
M80
C70

Y100
M70

Y70
M70
C100

871

Y100
M80
C80

Y20
C100

Y20
M80
C60
BL50

868

M40
C50
BL60

M80
C70

Y70
C100
BL80

872

Y100
C100
BL30

Y100
M100

Y30
M100
C100
BL20

Vivid Color plus
Concentrated Colors (2)
In this contrast, two concentrated colors
are placed with one brilliant color. This
combination is hard to use because the
brighter color tends to be overpowering.
To control the effect, change the proportions of the colors.

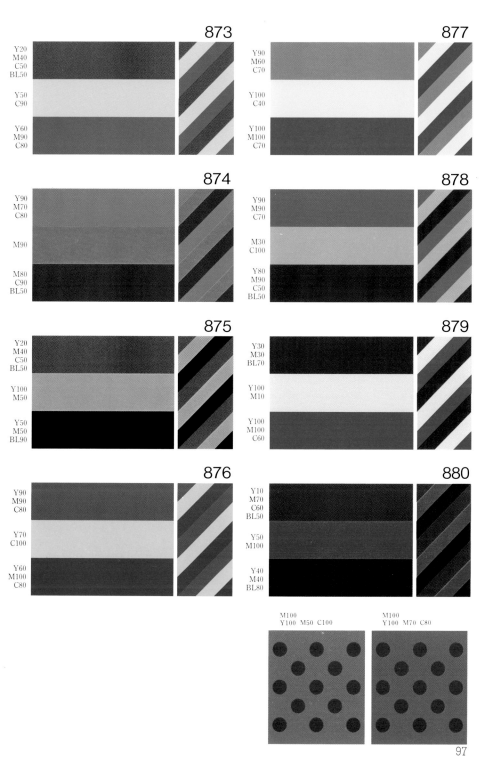

873

Y20
M40
C50
BL50

Y50
C90

Y60
M90
C80

874

Y90
M70
C80

M90

M80
C90
BL50

875

Y20
M40
C50
BL50

Y100
M50

Y50
M50
BL90

876

Y90
M90
C80

Y70
C100

Y60
M100
C80

877

Y90
M60
C70

Y100
C40

Y100
M100
C70

878

Y90
M90
C70

M30
C100

Y80
M90
C50
BL50

879

Y30
M30
BL70

Y100
M10

Y100
M100
C60

880

Y10
M70
C60
BL50

Y50
M100

Y40
M40
BL80

M100
Y100 M50 C100

M100
Y100 M70 C80

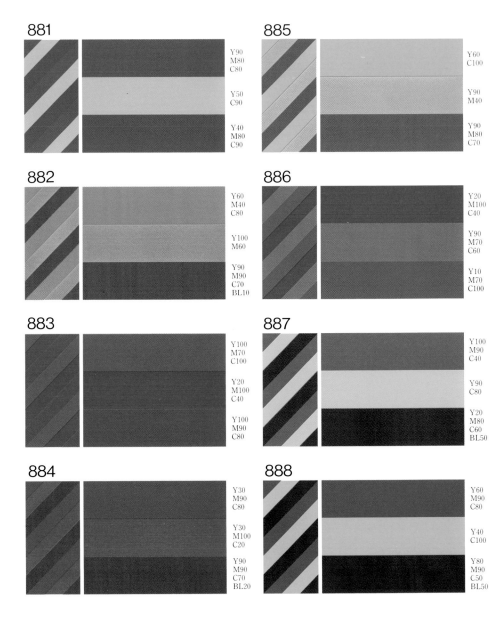

881

Y90
M80
C80

Y50
C90

Y40
M80
C90

885

Y60
C100

Y90
M40

Y90
M80
C70

882

Y60
M40
C80

Y100
M60

Y90
M90
C70
BL10

886

Y20
M100
C40

Y90
M70
C60

Y10
M70
C100

883

Y100
M70
C100

Y20
M100
C40

Y100
M90
C80

887

Y100
M90
C40

Y90
C80

Y20
M80
C60
BL50

884

Y30
M90
C80

Y30
M100
C20

Y90
M90
C70
BL20

888

Y60
M90
C80

Y40
C100

Y80
M90
C50
BL50

Deep Colors (1)
These color schemes are similar in color
and brightness to those on the previous
two pages. In general, these have an appealing folk-art and folk-craft look.

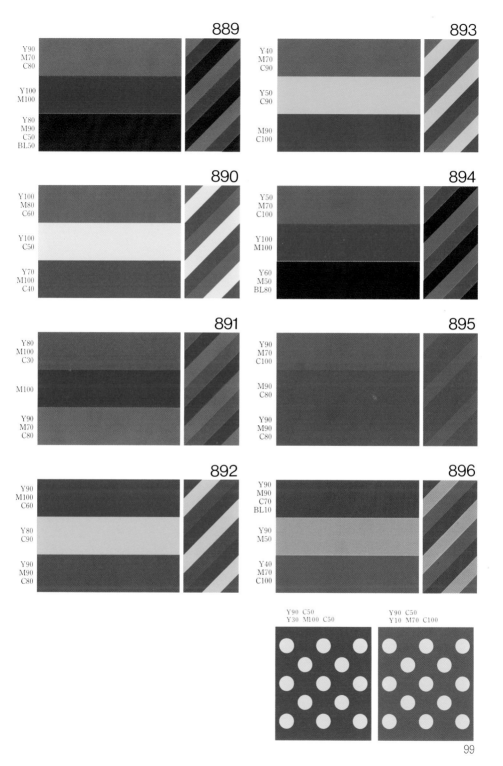

889

Y90
M70
C80

Y100
M100

Y80
M90
C50
BL50

890

Y100
M80
C60

Y100
C50

Y70
M100
C40

891

Y80
M100
C30

M100

Y90
M70
C80

892

Y90
M100
C60

Y80
C90

Y90
M90
C80

893

Y40
M70
C90

Y50
C90

M90
C100

894

Y50
M70
C100

Y100
M100

Y60
M50
BL80

895

Y90
M70
C100

M90
C80

Y90
M90
C80

896

Y90
M90
C70
BL10

Y90
M50

Y40
M70
C100

Y90 C50
Y30 M100 C50

Y90 C50
Y10 M70 C100

99

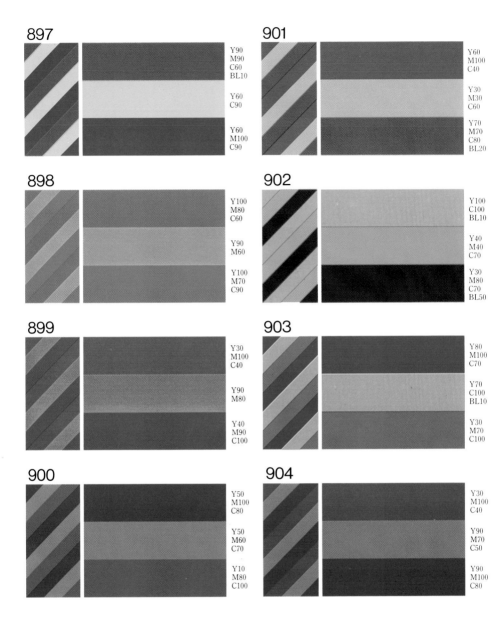

897

Y90
M90
C60
BL10

Y60
C90

Y60
M100
C90

901

Y60
M100
C40

Y30
M30
C60

Y70
M70
C80
BL20

898

Y100
M80
C60

Y90
M60

Y100
M70
C90

902

Y100
C100
BL10

Y40
M40
C70

Y30
M80
C70
BL50

899

Y30
M100
C40

Y90
M80

Y40
M90
C100

903

Y80
M100
C70

Y70
C100
BL10

Y30
M70
C100

900

Y50
M100
C80

Y50
M60
C70

Y10
M80
C100

904

Y30
M100
C40

Y90
M70
C50

Y90
M100
C80

Deep Colors (2)
The quietness and a certain degree of
brightness in these combinations tell of
approaching autumn.

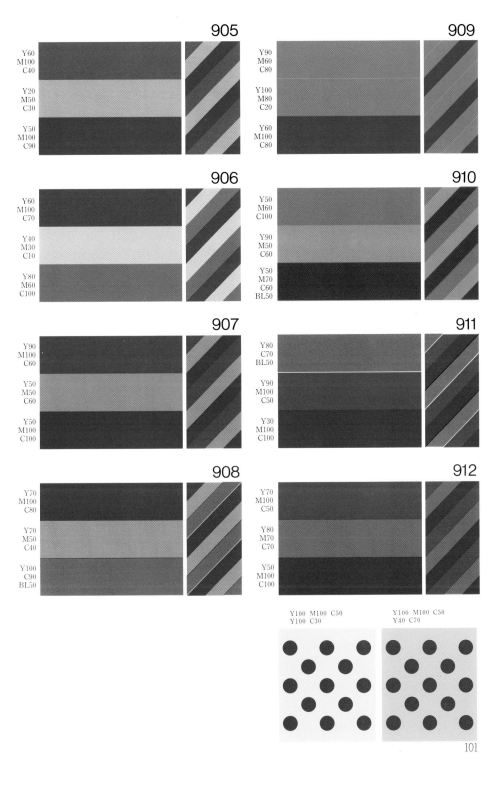

905

Y60
M100
C40

Y20
M50
C30

Y50
M100
C90

909

Y90
M60
C80

Y100
M80
C20

Y60
M100
C80

906

Y60
M100
C70

Y40
M30
C10

Y80
M60
C100

910

Y50
M60
C100

Y90
M50
C60

Y50
M70
C60
BL50

907

Y90
M100
C60

Y50
M50
C60

Y50
M100
C100

911

Y80
C70
BL50

Y90
M100
C50

Y30
M100
C100

908

Y70
M100
C80

Y70
M50
C40

Y100
C90
BL50

912

Y70
M100
C50

Y80
M70
C70

Y50
M100
C100

Y100 M100 C50
Y100 C30

Y100 M100 C50
Y40 C70

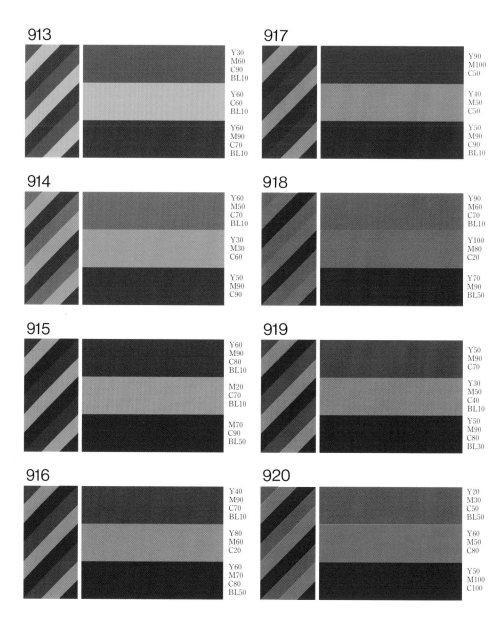

913
Y30 M60 C90 BL10
Y60 C60 BL10
Y60 M90 C70 BL10

917
Y90 M100 C50
Y40 M50 C50
Y50 M90 C90 BL10

914
Y60 M50 C70 BL10
Y30 M30 C60
Y50 M90 C90

918
Y90 M60 C70 BL10
Y100 M80 C20
Y70 M90 BL50

915
Y60 M90 C80 BL10
M20 C70 BL10
M70 C90 BL50

919
Y50 M90 C70
Y30 M50 C40 BL10
Y50 M90 C80 BL30

916
Y40 M90 C70 BL10
Y80 M60 C20
Y60 M70 C80 BL50

920
Y20 M30 C50 BL50
Y60 M50 C80
Y50 M100 C100

Deep Colors (3)
This third sequence of deep colors puts slightly dull colors into combinations that have a wide number of uses. If all three tones are equally strong, the result can seem fashion oriented. Making one color stronger will serve as an accent.

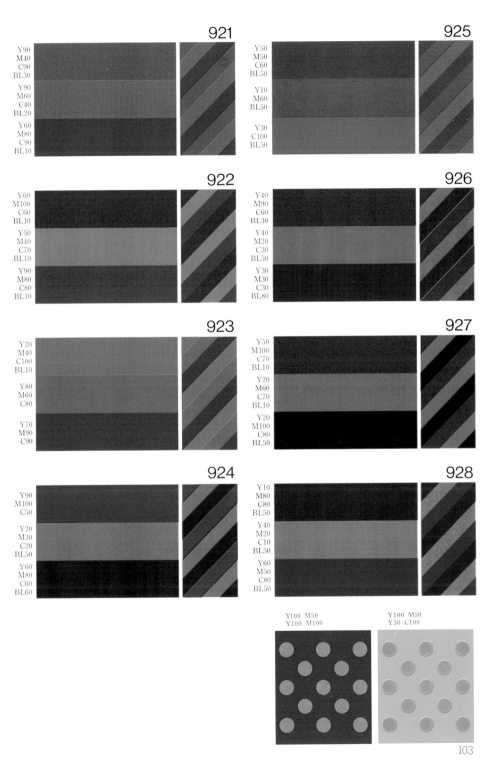

921

Y90 M40 C90 BL30
Y90 M60 C40 BL20
Y60 M80 C90 BL10

925

Y50 M50 C60 BL50
Y10 M60 BL50
Y30 C100 BL50

922

Y60 M100 C60 BL10
Y50 M40 C70 BL10
Y90 M80 C80 BL10

926

Y40 M90 C60 BL30
Y40 M20 C30 BL50
Y30 M30 C30 BL80

923

Y20 M40 C100 BL10
Y80 M60 C80
Y70 M90 C90

927

Y50 M100 C70 BL10
Y20 M60 C70 BL10
Y20 M100 C80 BL50

924

Y90 M100 C50
Y20 M30 C20 BL50
Y60 M80 C60 BL60

928

Y10 M80 C80 BL50
Y40 M20 C10 BL50
Y60 M50 C80 BL50

Y100 M50
Y100 M100

Y100 M50
Y50 C100

103

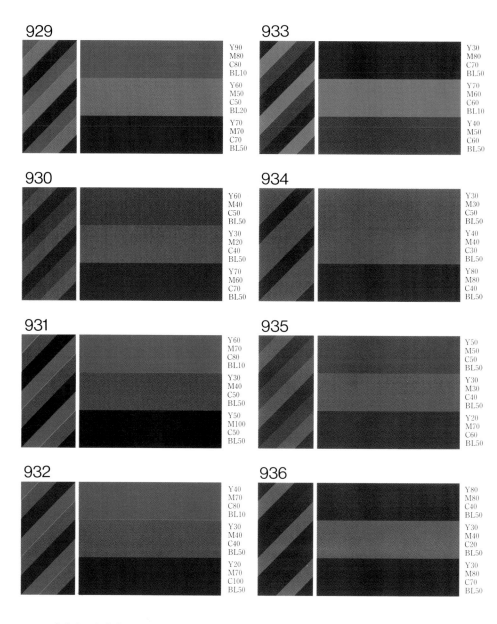

929
Y90 M80 C80 BL10
Y60 M50 C50 BL20
Y70 M70 C70 BL50

933
Y30 M80 C70 BL50
Y70 M60 C60 BL10
Y40 M50 C60 BL50

930
Y60 M40 C50 BL50
Y30 M20 C40 BL50
Y70 M60 C70 BL50

934
Y30 M30 C50 BL50
Y40 M40 C30 BL50
Y80 M80 C40 BL50

931
Y60 M70 C80 BL10
Y30 M40 C50 BL50
Y50 M100 C50 BL50

935
Y50 M50 C50 BL50
Y30 M30 C40 BL50
Y20 M70 C60 BL50

932
Y40 M70 C80 BL10
Y30 M40 C40 BL50
Y20 M70 C100 BL50

936
Y80 M80 C40 BL50
Y30 M40 C20 BL50
Y30 M80 C70 BL50

Dark Subdued Colors
In selecting these darker, subdued colors,
keep in mind the emotional signals you
may want to send. If you want to suppress
the color, choose similar tones and
thereby increase their darkness or dull-
ness. Compared to other color schemes,
they may seem gloomy, but they've been
applied very successfully in fashion.

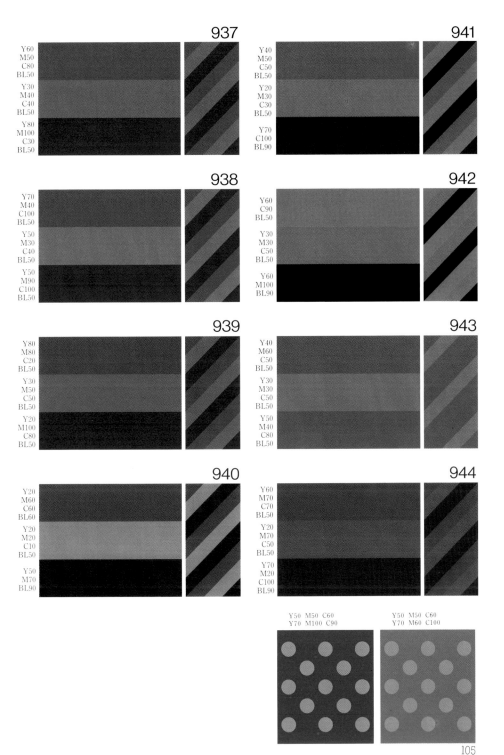

937

Y60 M50 C80 BL50
Y30 M40 C40 BL50
Y80 M100 C30 BL50

941

Y40 M50 C50 BL50
Y20 M30 C30 BL50
Y70 C100 BL90

938

Y70 M40 C100 BL50
Y50 M30 C40 BL50
Y50 M90 C100 BL50

942

Y60 C90 BL50
Y30 M30 C50 BL50
Y60 M100 BL90

939

Y80 M80 C20 BL50
Y30 M50 C50 BL50
Y20 M100 C80 BL50

943

Y40 M60 C50 BL50
Y30 M30 C50 BL50
Y50 M40 C80 BL50

940

Y20 M60 C60 BL60
Y20 M20 C10 BL50
Y50 M70 BL90

944

Y60 M70 C70 BL50
Y20 M70 C50 BL50
Y70 M20 C100 BL90

Y50 M50 C60
Y70 M100 C90

Y50 M50 C60
Y70 M60 C100

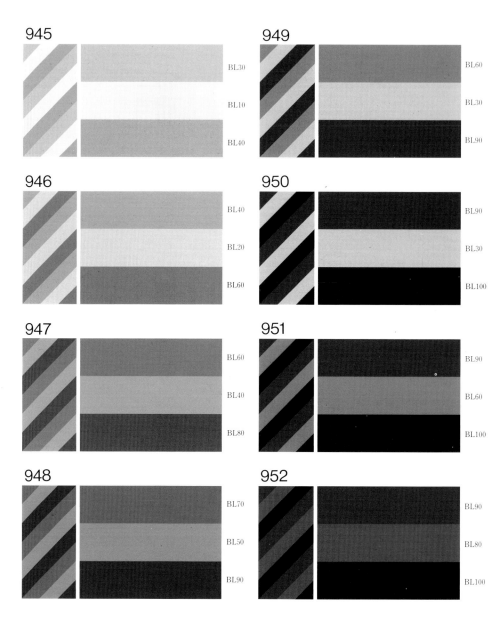

945

BL30
BL10
BL40

949

BL60
BL30
BL90

946

BL40
BL20
BL60

950

BL90
BL30
BL100

947

BL60
BL40
BL80

951

BL90
BL60
BL100

948

BL70
BL50
BL90

952

BL90
BL80
BL100

Black–Gray–White

Between black and white are the very
versatile grays, covering a full range of
brightness; still, it is difficult to imagine a
scheme made up of only "colorless" grays.
Gray offers a contrast in brightness, and
with black and white it is a basic color in
interior and environmental design and
fashion.

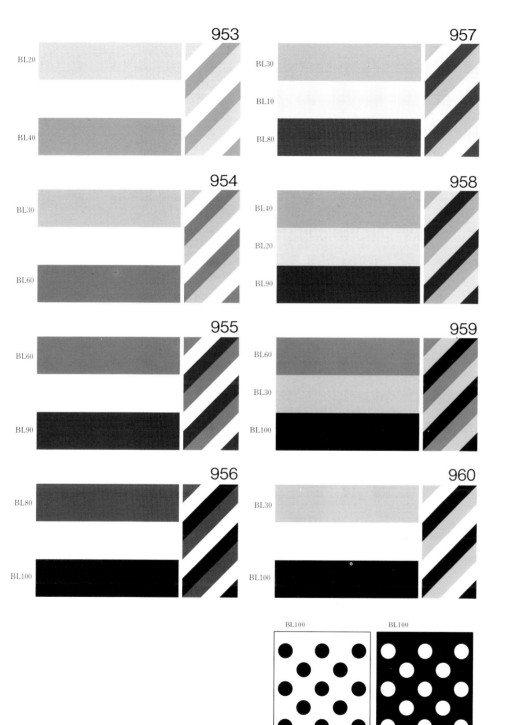

953

BL20

BL40

957

BL30

BL10

BL80

954

BL30

BL60

958

BL40

BL20

BL90

955

BL60

BL90

959

BL60

BL30

BL100

956

BL80

BL100

960

BL30

BL100

BL100

BL100

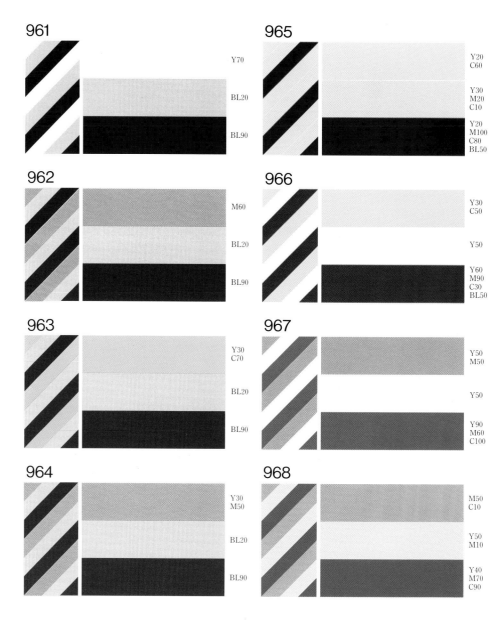

961
Y70
BL20
BL90

965
Y20
C60
Y30
M20
C10
Y20
M100
C80
BL50

962
M60
BL20
BL90

966
Y30
C50
Y50
Y60
M90
C30
BL50

963
Y30
C70
BL20
BL90

967
Y50
M50
Y50
Y90
M60
C100

964
Y30
M50
BL20
BL90

968
M50
C10
Y50
M10
Y40
M70
C90

Effects of Contrast (1)
These examples contain two light colors
and one dark color. They suggest Ha-
waiian shirts, calypso music, and offbeat
tropical settings.

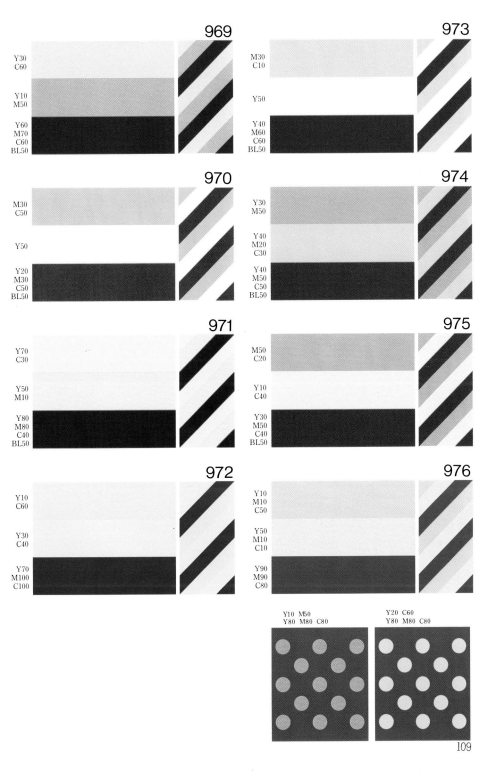

969

Y30
C60

Y10
M50

Y60
M70
C60
BL50

970

M30
C50

Y50

Y20
M30
C50
BL50

971

Y70
C30

Y50
M10

Y80
M80
C40
BL50

972

Y10
C60

Y30
C40

Y70
M100
C100

973

M30
C10

Y50

Y40
M60
C60
BL50

974

Y30
M50

Y40
M20
C30

Y40
M50
C50
BL50

975

M50
C20

Y10
C40

Y30
M50
C40
BL50

976

Y10
M10
C50

Y50
M10
C10

Y90
M90
C80

Y10 M50
Y80 M80 C80

Y20 C60
Y80 M80 C80

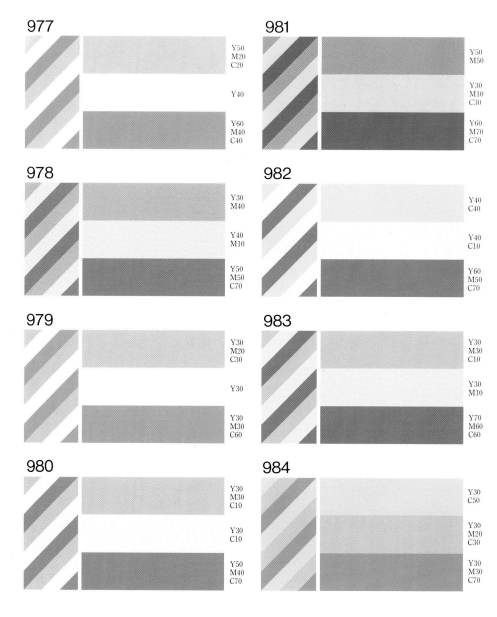

977

Y50 M20 C20

Y40

Y60 M40 C40

981

Y50 M50

Y30 M10 C30

Y60 M70 C70

978

Y30 M40

Y40 M10

Y50 M50 C70

982

Y40 C40

Y40 C10

Y60 M50 C70

979

Y30 M20 C30

Y30

Y30 M30 C60

983

Y30 M30 C10

Y30 M10

Y70 M60 C60

980

Y30 M30 C10

Y30 C10

Y50 M40 C70

984

Y30 C50

Y30 M20 C30

Y30 M30 C70

Effects of Contrast (2)
Color schemes on these pages are based on colors that are somewhat softer than those on the preceding pages. The differences in bright and quiet colors result in color groupings more suitable for interior design than fabric or fashion.

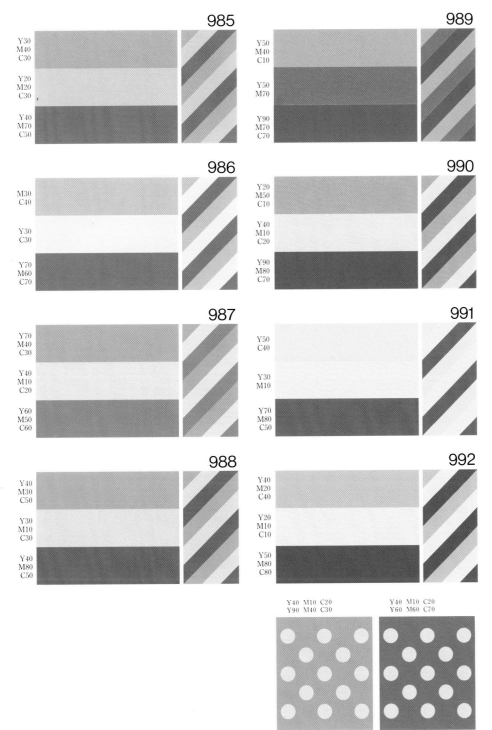

985

Y30 M40 C30

Y20 M20 C30

Y40 M70 C50

989

Y50 M40 C10

Y50 M70

Y90 M70 C70

986

M30 C40

Y30 C30

Y70 M60 C70

990

Y20 M50 C10

Y40 M10 C20

Y90 M80 C70

987

Y70 M40 C30

Y40 M10 C20

Y60 M50 C60

991

Y50 C40

Y30 M10

Y70 M80 C50

988

Y40 M30 C50

Y30 M10 C30

Y40 M80 C50

992

Y40 M20 C40

Y20 M10 C10

Y50 M80 C80

Y40 M10 C20
Y90 M40 C30

Y40 M10 C20
Y60 M60 C70

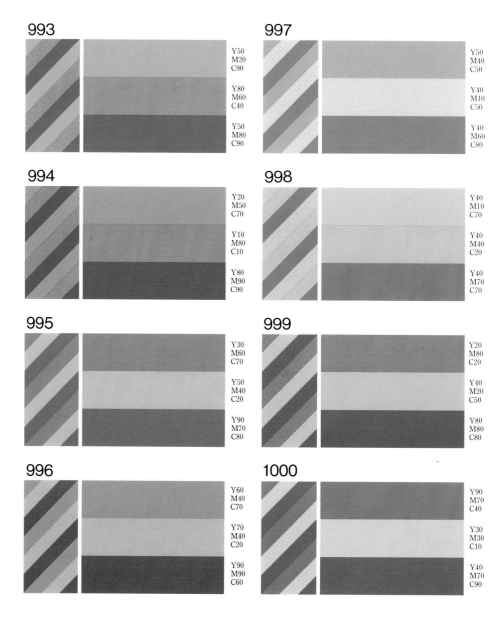

993

Y50 M20 C90

Y80 M60 C40

Y50 M80 C90

997

Y50 M40 C50

Y40 M10 C50

Y40 M60 C80

994

Y20 M50 C70

Y10 M80 C10

Y80 M90 C90

998

Y40 M10 C70

Y40 M40 C20

Y40 M70 C70

995

Y30 M60 C70

Y50 M40 C20

Y90 M70 C80

999

Y20 M80 C20

Y40 M20 C50

Y80 M80 C80

996

Y60 M40 C70

Y70 M40 C20

Y90 M90 C60

1000

Y90 M70 C40

Y30 M30 C10

Y40 M70 C90

Free Color Schemes (1)
These are mid-range colors arranged for a pleasant, restful effect. The combinations can be widely used, from fashion to interior design.

112

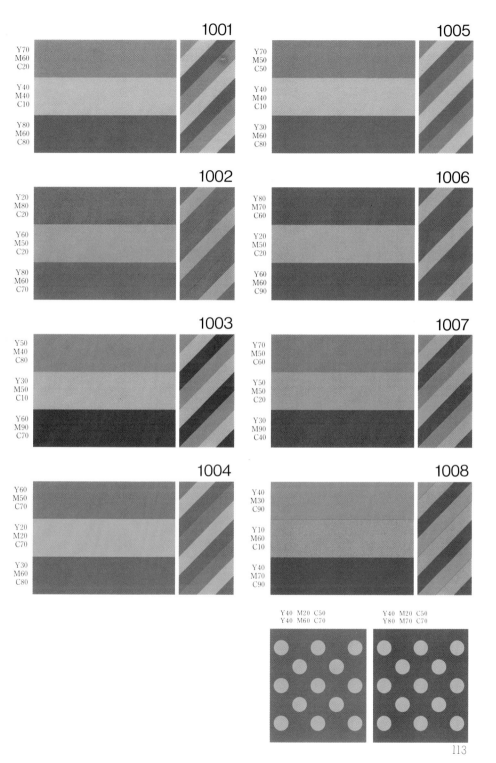

1001

Y70
M60
C20

Y40
M40
C10

Y80
M60
C80

1002

Y20
M80
C20

Y60
M50
C20

Y80
M60
C70

1003

Y50
M40
C80

Y30
M50
C10

Y60
M90
C70

1004

Y60
M50
C70

Y20
M20
C70

Y30
M60
C80

1005

Y70
M50
C50

Y40
M40
C10

Y30
M60
C80

1006

Y80
M70
C60

Y20
M50
C20

Y60
M60
C90

1007

Y70
M50
C60

Y50
M50
C20

Y30
M90
C40

1008

Y40
M30
C90

Y10
M60
C10

Y40
M70
C90

Y40 M20 C50
Y40 M60 C70

Y40 M20 C50
Y80 M70 C70

113

1009
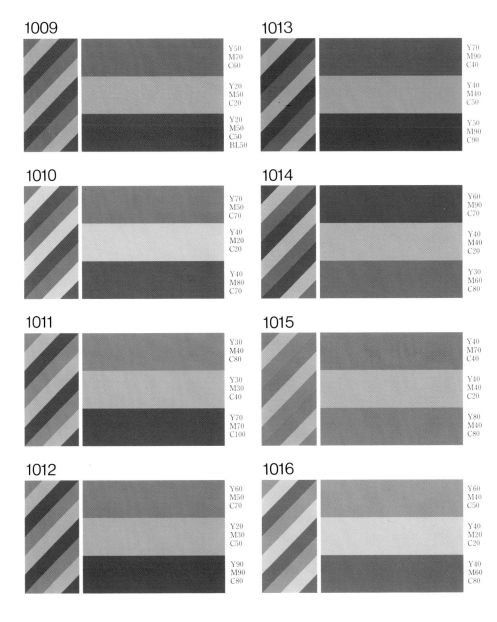

Y50
M70
C60

Y20
M50
C20

Y20
M50
C50
BL50

1013

Y70
M90
C40

Y40
M40
C50

Y50
M90
C90

1010

Y70
M50
C70

Y40
M20
C20

Y40
M80
C70

1014

Y60
M90
C70

Y40
M40
C20

Y30
M60
C80

1011

Y30
M40
C80

Y30
M30
C40

Y70
M70
C100

1015

Y40
M70
C40

Y40
M40
C20

Y80
M40
C80

1012

Y60
M50
C70

Y20
M30
C50

Y90
M90
C80

1016

Y60
M40
C50

Y40
M20
C20

Y40
M60
C80

Free Color Schemes (continued)

114

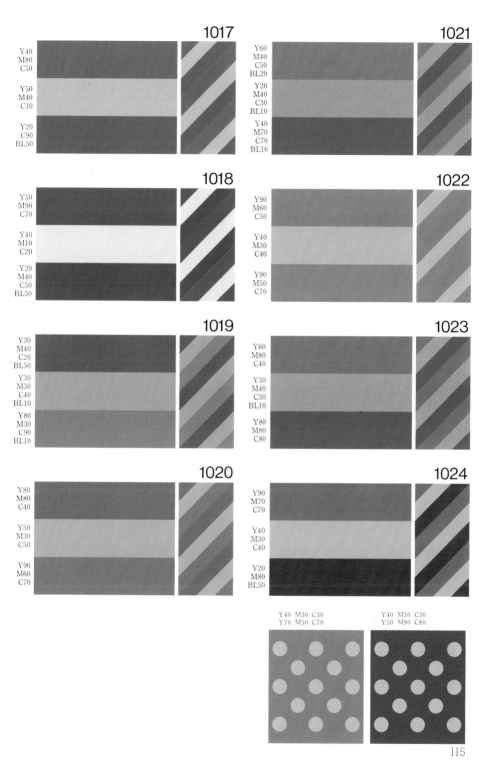

1017

Y40
M80
C50

Y50
M40
C10

Y20
C90
BL50

1021

Y60
M40
C50
BL20

Y20
M40
C30
BL10

Y40
M70
C70
BL10

1018

Y50
M90
C70

Y40
M10
C20

Y20
M40
C50
BL50

1022

Y90
M60
C50

Y40
M30
C40

Y90
M50
C70

1019

Y30
M40
C20
BL50

Y30
M30
C40
BL10

Y80
M30
C90
BL10

1023

Y60
M80
C40

Y30
M40
C30
BL10

Y80
M80
C80

1020

Y80
M80
C40

Y50
M30
C50

Y90
M60
C70

1024

Y90
M70
C70

Y40
M30
C40

Y20
M80
BL50

Y40 M30 C30
Y70 M50 C70

Y40 M30 C30
Y50 M90 C80

115

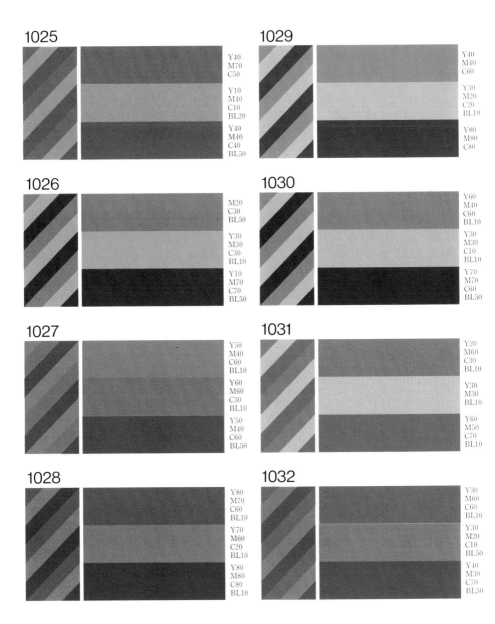

1025
Y40
M70
C50

Y10
M40
C10
BL20

Y40
M40
C40
BL50

1026
M20
C30
BL50

Y30
M30
C30
BL10

Y10
M70
C70
BL50

1027
Y50
M40
C60
BL10

Y60
M60
C30
BL10

Y50
M40
C60
BL50

1028
Y80
M70
C60
BL10

Y70
M60
C20
BL10

Y80
M80
C80
BL10

1029
Y40
M40
C60

Y30
M20
C20
BL10

Y80
M80
C80

1030
Y60
M40
C60
BL10

Y30
M30
C10
BL10

Y70
M70
C60
BL50

1031
Y20
M60
C30
BL10

Y30
M30
BL10

Y60
M50
C70
BL10

1032
Y30
M60
C60
BL10

Y30
M20
C10
BL50

Y40
M30
C70
BL50

Free Color Schemes (2)
Using three smoky, subdued colors produces natural and quiet color schemes full
of earth tones—subtle, graceful, and
quiet.

116

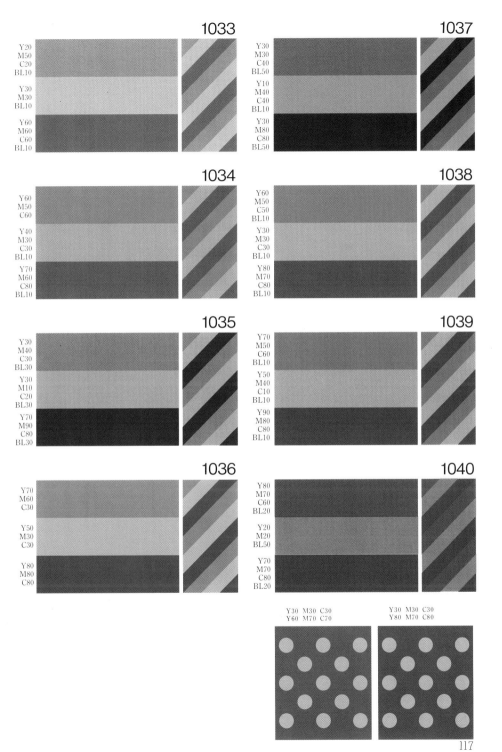

1033

Y20
M50
C20
BL10

Y30
M30
BL10

Y60
M60
C60
BL10

1034

Y60
M50
C60

Y40
M30
C30
BL10

Y70
M60
C80
BL10

1035

Y30
M40
C30
BL30

Y30
M10
C20
BL30

Y70
M90
C80
BL30

1036

Y70
M60
C30

Y50
M30
C30

Y80
M80
C80

1037

Y30
M30
C40
BL50

Y10
M40
C40
BL10

Y30
M80
C80
BL50

1038

Y60
M50
C50
BL10

Y30
M30
C30
BL10

Y80
M70
C80
BL10

1039

Y70
M50
C60
BL10

Y50
M40
C10
BL10

Y90
M80
C80
BL10

1040

Y80
M70
C60
BL20

Y20
M20
BL50

Y70
M70
C80
BL20

Y30 M30 C30
Y60 M70 C70

Y30 M30 C30
Y80 M70 C80

117

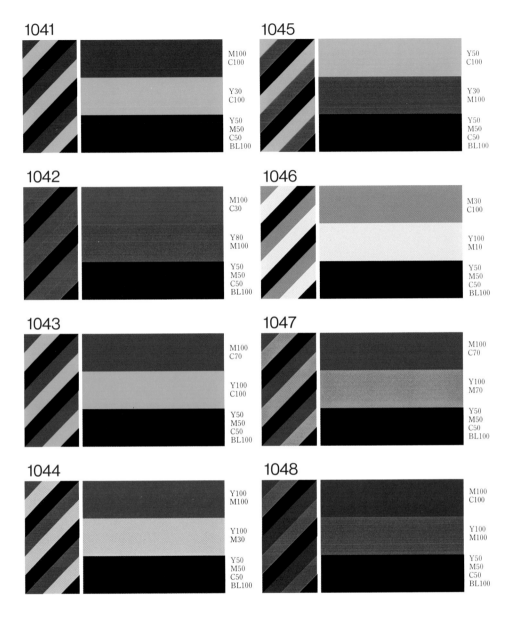

1041

M100
C100

Y30
C100

Y50
M50
C50
BL100

1042

M100
C30

Y80
M100

Y50
M50
C50
BL100

1043

M100
C70

Y100
C100

Y50
M50
C50
BL100

1044

Y100
M100

Y100
M30

Y50
M50
C50
BL100

1045

Y50
C100

Y30
M100

Y50
M50
C50
BL100

1046

M30
C100

Y100
M10

Y50
M50
C50
BL100

1047

M100
C70

Y100
M70

Y50
M50
C50
BL100

1048

M100
C100

Y100
M100

Y50
M50
C50
BL100

Black and Vivid Colors
Again, the addition of black is always
striking and dramatic. This page demon-
strates the graphic power of combining
equal proportions of two strong colors and
black.

118

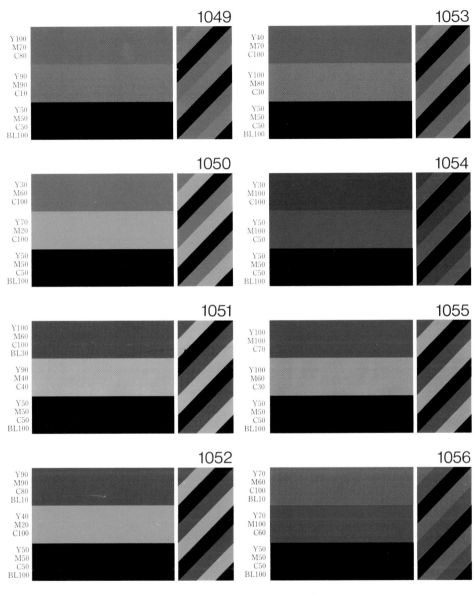

1049
Y100
M70
C80

Y90
M90
C10

Y50
M50
C50
BL100

1053
Y40
M70
C100

Y100
M80
C30

Y50
M50
C50
BL100

1050
Y30
M60
C100

Y70
M20
C100

Y50
M50
C50
BL100

1054
Y30
M100
C100

Y50
M100
C50

Y50
M50
C50
BL100

1051
Y100
M60
C100
BL30

Y90
M40
C40

Y50
M50
C50
BL100

1055
Y100
M100
C70

Y100
M60
C30

Y50
M50
C50
BL100

1052
Y90
M90
C80
BL10

Y40
M20
C100

Y50
M50
C50
BL100

1056
Y70
M60
C100
BL10

Y70
M100
C60

Y50
M50
C50
BL100

Black and Deep Colors
Combined with more somber colors black intensifies their depth and richness.

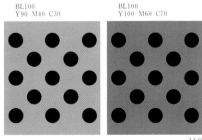

BL100
Y90 M40 C30

BL100
Y100 M60 C70

119

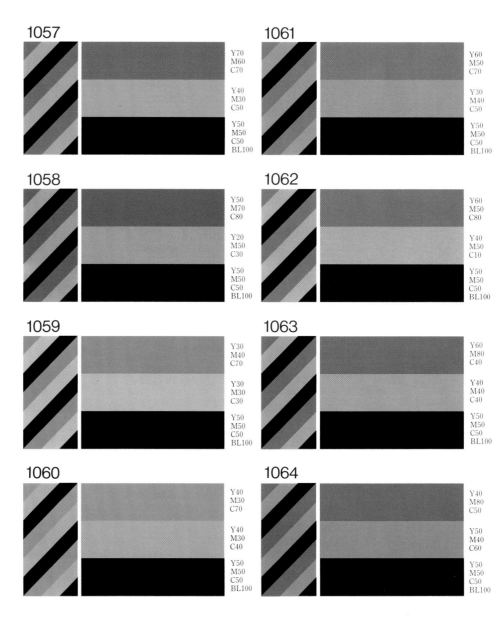

1057

Y70
M60
C70

Y40
M30
C50

Y50
M50
C50
BL100

1061

Y60
M50
C70

Y30
M40
C50

Y50
M50
C50
BL100

1058

Y50
M70
C80

Y20
M50
C30

Y50
M50
C50
BL100

1062

Y60
M50
C80

Y40
M50
C10

Y50
M50
C50
BL100

1059

Y30
M40
C70

Y30
M30
C30

Y50
M50
C50
BL100

1063

Y60
M80
C40

Y40
M40
C40

Y50
M50
C50
BL100

1060

Y40
M30
C70

Y40
M30
C40

Y50
M50
C50
BL100

1064

Y40
M80
C50

Y50
M40
C60

Y50
M50
C50
BL100

Black and Medium Colors

Next to these restrained colors, black becomes dominant and the resulting color scheme is sophisticated and fashionable. Medium colors are basically soft; black has a bracing effect and helps to define them.

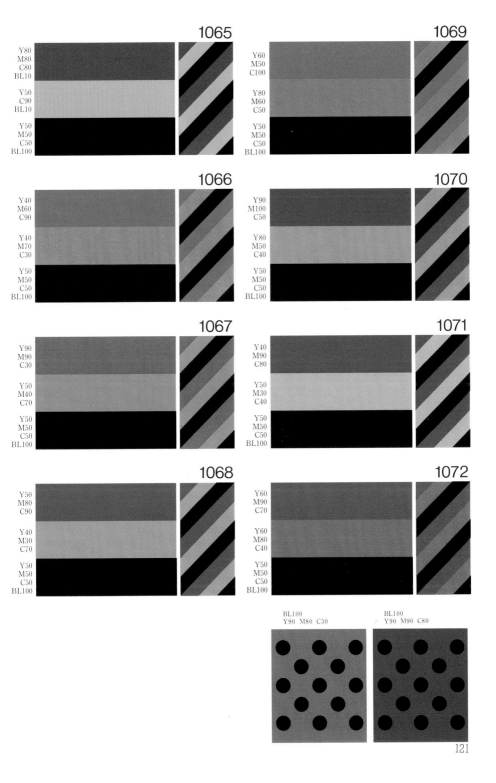

1065
Y80 M80 C80 BL10
Y50 C90 BL10
Y50 M50 C50 BL100

1069
Y60 M50 C100
Y80 M60 C50
Y50 M50 C50 BL100

1066
Y40 M60 C90
Y40 M70 C30
Y50 M50 C50 BL100

1070
Y90 M100 C50
Y80 M50 C40
Y50 M50 C50 BL100

1067
Y90 M90 C30
Y50 M40 C70
Y50 M50 C50 BL100

1071
Y40 M90 C80
Y50 M30 C40
Y50 M50 C50 BL100

1068
Y50 M80 C90
Y40 M30 C70
Y50 M50 C50 BL100

1072
Y60 M90 C70
Y60 M80 C40
Y50 M50 C50 BL100

BL100
Y90 M80 C30

BL100
Y90 M90 C80

121

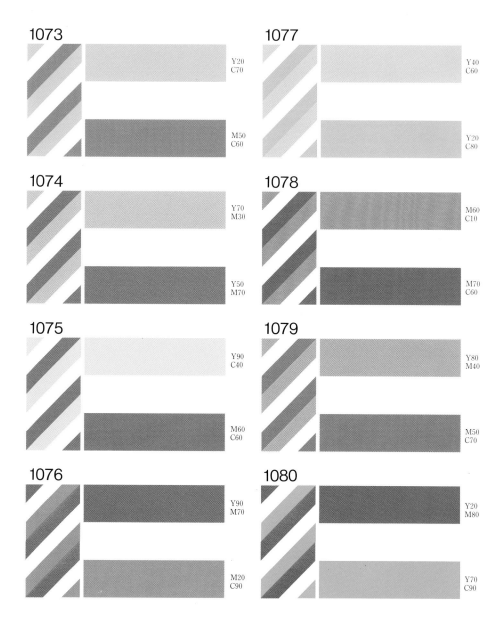

1073

Y20
C70

M50
C60

1077

Y40
C60

Y20
C80

1074

Y70
M30

Y50
M70

1078

M60
C10

M70
C60

1075

Y90
C40

M60
C60

1079

Y80
M40

M50
C70

1076

Y90
M70

M20
C90

1080

Y20
M80

Y70
C90

White with Vivid Colors
Adding white both brightens and lightens
color schemes. This results in combinations that are sporty and refreshing.
These examples evoke flag images as
well.

122

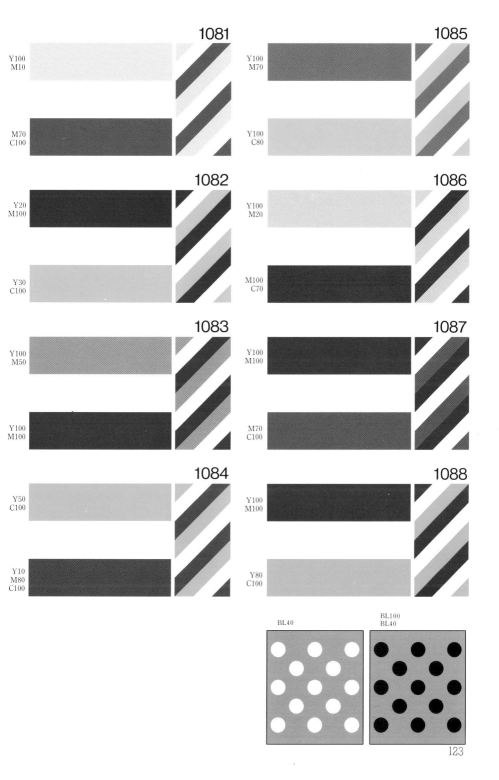

1081
Y100 M10
M70 C100

1085
Y100 M70
Y100 C80

1082
Y20 M100
Y30 C100

1086
Y100 M20
M100 C70

1083
Y100 M50
Y100 M100

1087
Y100 M100
M70 C100

1084
Y50 C100
Y10 M80 C100

1088
Y100 M100
Y80 C100

BL40

BL100 BL40

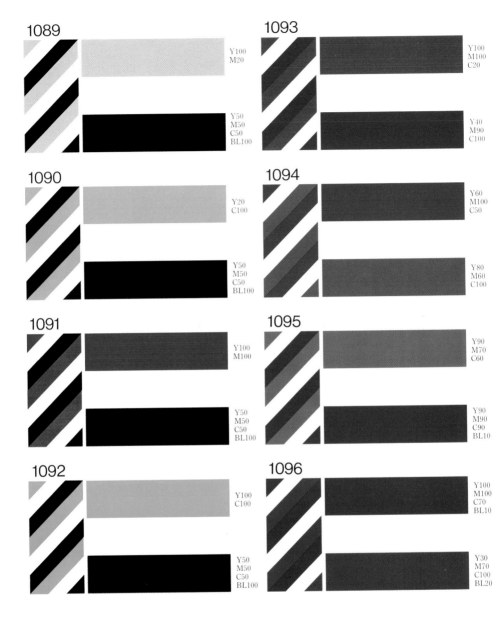

1089

Y100
M20

Y50
M50
C50
BL100

1090

Y20
C100

Y50
M50
C50
BL100

1091

Y100
M100

Y50
M50
C50
BL100

1092

Y100
C100

Y50
M50
C50
BL100

1093

Y100
M100
C20

Y40
M90
C100

1094

Y60
M100
C50

Y80
M60
C100

1095

Y90
M70
C60

Y90
M90
C90
BL10

1096

Y100
M100
C70
BL10

Y30
M70
C100
BL20

White with Other Colors

Like those on the previous two pages,
these color schemes are lighter because
of the addition of white. Substituting gray
or beige for white is often too powerful
and may destroy tonal harmony.

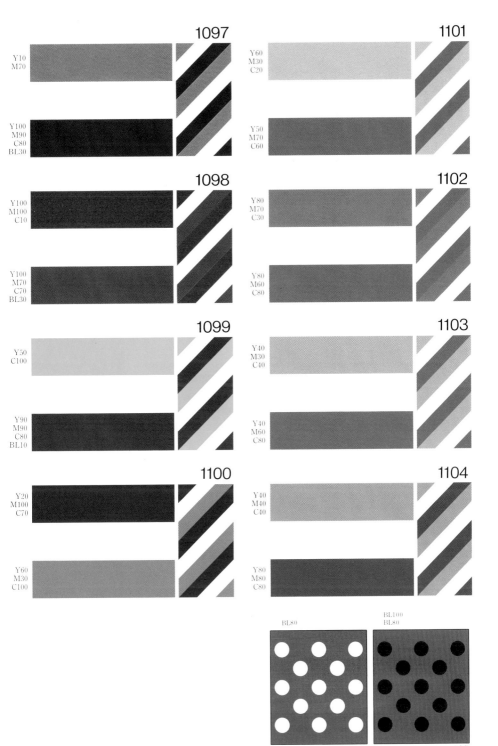

1097

Y10
M70

Y100
M90
C80
BL30

1098

Y100
M100
C10

Y100
M70
C70
BL30

1099

Y50
C100

Y90
M90
C80
BL10

1100

Y20
M100
C70

Y60
M30
C100

1101

Y60
M30
C20

Y50
M70
C60

1102

Y80
M70
C30

Y80
M60
C80

1103

Y40
M30
C40

Y40
M60
C80

1104

Y40
M40
C40

Y80
M80
C80

BL80

BL100
BL80

125

Concentration Scale

Y

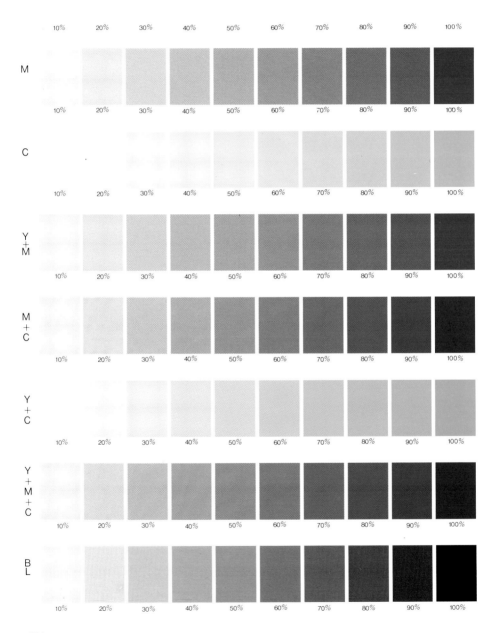

M

C

Y
+
M

M
+
C

Y
+
C

Y
+
M
+
C

B
L

bright

| Y50 | Y50 C10 | Y50 C20 | Y50 C30 | Y50 C50 | Y30 C50 | Y20 C50 | Y10 C50 | C50 | M10 C50 |

| M30 C50 | M50 C50 | M50 C30 | M50 C10 | M50 | Y10 M50 | Y30 M50 | Y50 M50 | Y50 M30 | Y50 M10 |

vivid

| Y100 | Y100 C30 | Y100 C70 | Y100 C100 | Y70 C100 | Y30 C100 | C100 | M20 C100 | M50 C100 | M70 C100 |

| M100 C100 | M100 C70 | M100 C50 | M100 C20 | M100 | Y30 M100 | Y70 M100 | Y100 M100 | Y100 M70 | Y100 M30 |

deep

| Y100 BL50 | Y100 C30 BL50 | Y100 C70 BL50 | Y100 C100 BL50 | Y70 C100 BL50 | Y30 C100 BL50 | C100 BL50 | M20 C100 BL50 | M50 C100 BL50 | M70 C100 BL50 |

| M100 C100 BL50 | M100 C70 BL50 | M100 C50 BL50 | M100 C20 BL50 | M100 BL50 | Y30 M100 BL50 | Y70 M100 BL50 | Y100 M100 BL50 | Y100 M70 BL50 | Y100 M30 BL50 |

grayish

| Y50 BL30 | Y50 C10 BL30 | Y50 C20 BL30 | Y50 C30 BL30 | Y50 C50 BL30 | Y30 C50 BL30 | Y20 C50 BL30 | Y10 C50 BL30 | C50 BL30 | M10 C50 BL30 |

| M30 C50 BL30 | M50 C50 BL30 | M50 C30 BL30 | M50 C10 BL30 | M50 BL30 | Y10 M50 BL30 | Y30 M50 BL30 | Y50 M50 BL30 | Y50 M30 BL30 | Y50 M10 BL30 |